Drinking the Wind

At the Limits of Endurance

Drinking the Wind

At the Limits of Endurance

John Tytler Thomson

Metal Rabbit Edition, Peebles

First published in Great Britain 2010

This revised edition published by
Metal Rabbit Editions 2011

A CIP Catalogue record for this book is available from the
British Library.

ISBN **978-0-9560415-2-4**

Printed and bound by CPI Antony Rowe,
Chippenham and Eastbourne, England.

Drinking the Wind – "His book about his 200 mile Trans Scotland ride is an entertaining read. It had me laughing and crying, holding my breath and sighing with relief as I felt I was riding along side him with every page.

For me John can take his place alongside the likes of Bob Champion and Lance Armstrong. Men who when faced with life threatening illnesses have used their sport as a battle ground to fight back. Proving that they will not be beaten and "normal" life will continue.

The book is full of colourful descriptions of the scenery, places and people Team Omar encounter on route, as well as informative historical, geographical, botanical, theological and literary references. Clearly a lot of research has gone into producing this rounded and enjoyable read." *Nikki Pearson, EGB Cumbria Branch Secretary*

"I have just finished reading the book. Feeling rather emotional and overwhelmed to be honest. So inspirational! Such an achievement! He must be so proud of Omar and what has been done. It tells of the bond between a horse and human that is so precious and a real treasure." *Lynn Healey, Culgarth*

"I was drawn in from the very beginning. The story is so life affirming and encouraging." *Kathy Low, Dundee*

"This book is so emotionally charged in places I went through a box of tissues then found myself laughing hysterically at the wicked sense of humour. It is a remarkable story of a journey of achievement that anyone would be proud of. It is an inspiration. The description of the Scottish scenery, history and culture is breathtaking." *Lesley & Laurence, Bury St Edmonds*

"Awesome!! When is the movie coming out?" *Delores Wotring, South Carolina*

"This is a book which manages to be powerful and moving, inspiring and informative all together. It tells the reader a lot about the almost magical bond that can be formed between horse and rider and much about the historic country through which John passed. And it says much too about the invincibility of the human spirit. This book will have a strong US readership."
T Smith, London

The wind of heaven is that which blows between a horses ears.

ARABIAN PROVERB

Acknowledgements

Wow! It's finally finished and as my daughters Gemma and Victoria might say......."How cool is that!" Actually I am feeling quite pleased with myself because now I really can say a big thank you to all those people who provided encouragement and support throughout the last couple of years.

To my sister Muriel Prince and Metal Rabbit Editions, many thanks for smoothing the anachronistic path of publishing. To the very talented Jo McGrath and Don Nealon, I am indebted for the cover design and photograph. Many thanks also to Jason Masters for the use of his competitive photographs. To Sally Atkinson who worked me so hard in the school, I hope that I lived up to her expectations and to Candy Cameron for her tuition and encouragement. Thank you both so much.

For my crew, what can I say? A very special mention is due to Paul and Matt Thomson and Marc Millson for the hard work to get us through some very demanding stages. The use of their photographs is also greatly appreciated. Thanks guys!

Of course none of this might have been possible without my loyal buddy who is out chomping grass and about to be brought in for a wash and shampoo before another ride – the noble Prince Omar, a true son of the four winds.

But there is one person, a very special person that I owe the biggest debt of gratitude of all. Although I know that I can be difficult to live with sometimes and that her patience has been tried on too many occasions but her love, support and encouragement is endless and that is to my beautiful wife Rose.

Chapters

To Rose

This is for you

Out of the Shadows

"And I saw, and behold a white horse."

E ARLY summer sunlight was fading fast, the first
shadows of twilight starting to creep into the late
evening. Ironically, as the sun sank slowly into the
west, for the first time in my life, I was ready to give up.
Despite every conscious effort that I could think of it was
impossible to relax against the overwhelming tension that
was crashing through my fatigued body. Inside my chest I
could feel my heart pounding faster and faster, seemingly
out of control. A steady mounting numbness crept through
my left shoulder, running down my arm, across and into
the left side of my chest. Instinctively, I knew that my blood
pressure had raced past danger levels, placing me back into
a life threatening position. Surrounded by bright lights my
head ached, the noise of the medical support machines
exacerbating the confusion inside my tensed brain.
Although I desperately wanted to get up, the sheer mental
and physical fatigue that was draining my very soul, the
damage to my right leg and useless arm prevented me from
rising. I wanted to call for help but found it difficult to focus
on speech because the absolute effort was just too much.
My mind was absorbed in the concentration needed to fend
off the increasing tension; cardio stress induced by the

1

insidious brain damage that I knew was forcing my body to finally shut down.

As the icy fingers of death squeezed just a little bit tighter, sudden panic increased the anxiety. I tried to struggle from my bed but seemed to be frozen. Speech was impossible; as much as I tried nothing seemed to come from my vocal chords. My head was empty, confused, and impossible to clear. Any capability for logical reasoning was non-existent. An over-riding sensation of sheer blind panic started to set in. I wanted to get to a telephone to call my wife, ask her to come and take me home. I made a feeble struggle to get out of bed but was held, paralysed, some unseen weight holding me down. I desperately needed to be out of that place with the noise and bright lights, away from the sick and the dying but the confusion and cardio trauma continued. As much as I resisted, the weaker I seemed to become.

Another fleeting moment of mental dread set in. Again I thought of my wife at home, probably on the telephone speaking to the girls, letting them know how I was. I wanted to see them all, to hold their hands, to tell them that I loved them and to say a thousand things that I might never get the chance to ever say again. A sense of overwhelming urgency washed through me again. If this were to be my ultimate minutes on earth, I wanted one last chance to have the most important things around me.

There was an alarm button somewhere but I had no recollection of where it was located. Hoping that a telepathic message might alert someone I tried to focus my eyes on the nurses' desk, just out of sight at the end of the ward, but it was to no avail. Incredibly exhausted, I closed my eyes, took a long deep breath. Then for the first time in my life I let go, gave up. There was no further sense of consciousness. The next thing I knew, or seemed to waken into was a world of semi-darkness that was shrouded in mistiness along the peripheral edges. Lost, not sure of where I was or which direction I should be heading I strayed towards the hazy shadows. But something held me back.

Standing in the dimness, I turned my head left and right, my eyes searching. I stood in this murkiness, a shadowy world all around and stared into what seemed an impenetrable blackness. As my eyes accustomed to the gloom I had the distinct impression that I was in a dark tunnel. Unable to define any walls there still seemed to be a sense of curvature but it was too difficult to focus through the obscurity. In front of me, at the extremity of my vision where the mist seemed to swirl away from me, I could just barely define some shadows, eerie figures or shapes darting about the mistiness. For a moment I started towards them but some unknown force again seemed to hold me back. As I strained into an eerie gloominess, I no longer felt any sense of panic or dread; instead I became overwhelmed by a strange peace; of spiritual tranquillity, affection and well being yet tinged with a slight feeling of sadness.

I stood transfixed in the darkness, reluctant to move, still lost. Shadows danced and played ahead of me. For a moment I was again tempted to move towards the mistiness with its twisting shapes that seemed to be reaching towards me, beckoning me to join the throng. The temptation to reach out to the darting shapes became stronger but I resisted. Something, some force instructed me to stay still, avoid the temptation. I managed to eventually turn my head to my right then stared straight into what now could be clearly defined as a long black tunnel. Along the edges, the misty shapes moved around, flitting here and there, reaching out, calling me, and beckoning me to join them. Again I resisted. The line of the tunnel was clear, almost like a track, but oddly the shapes and shadows did not stray towards that centre line.

As I stared deeper into the shape of what appeared to be a passageway, I noticed something that seemed to be at a great distance away from me, a tiny speck of radiance. It was a minuscule flicker of light, a pinpoint lost in the dark world that surrounded it. But it was a glimmer of hope and I reckoned that if I moved towards the light I would be released from this dark world of emptiness with the eerie scurrying shapes that guarded the sides. Concentrating hard I focussed with my entire mind and might to move towards the pinpoint of iridescent illumination. The light mesmerised me but as hard as I tried I could not move any closer towards it. It seemed that I was stuck, firmly caught between the contradiction of darkness and light. As the dilemma of direction fashioned an impossible choice the shadowy figures on the peripheral of my vision danced closer, nearer, closer to touching me. As they did so it seemed as if the angels of death beckoned. Then an even stranger thing happened!

§

A few days beforehand life seemed to start as a typical mid week routine day. Up at my usual time around five o'clock I fumbled my way to the kitchen for a gulp of tea before taking Tig the dog for a walk through the fields. As I dressed that morning, I realised that my right arm and hand seemed to be weak, almost frozen, lacking in co-ordination. There was also a weakness, a sort of numbness, dead feeling in my right leg but shaking off any hint of concern put the feelings down to a poor sleeping posture. I had worked in the cloche the evening before, shifting compost, topping up the plants. Maybe I had pulled a muscle or trapped a nerve. Typically, as it had been a long day, I had probably slept well, the stiffness attributed to that. A nagging, numbing pain in the left side of my neck had been bothering me for a week or so but again I shrugged this off as I inevitably lay at an awkward angle on the pillows, assuming that the discomfort was of a purely musculature nature caused by a bad sleeping posture. By the time I returned to the house after a half hour's attempt at a brisk walk, the feeling in both my arm and leg had not diminished. I suspected something was wrong; certainly the growing emptiness, fuzziness inside my head was causing me just a little bit more concern than I wanted. This surprised me but I put the experience down to what I believed to be some sort of a muscle freeze, a kind of pins and needles, a flu bug maybe but fully expecting that the strength and feeling would return in time. It didn't!

After struggling through a shower and breakfast I left home at around 0645, heading for Alloa, a distance of some 85 miles, a good hour and a half drive. What I should have done was get to a hospital as fast as possible. As I drove through Dundee then on to Perth and the M90, I became gradually aware that something definitely wasn't quite right. Driving the Land Rover down the motorway towards the Kinross turn off, I was finding it increasingly difficult to keep my right foot from slipping off the accelerator pedal. For all purposes my foot was losing feeling as I applied pressure. Then as time wore on, the pressure required to keep my right foot in place became increasingly harder. It seemed that I had no control over what felt like a very clumsy foot. My concentration was also progressively deteriorating but somehow I managed to get to the office car park in Alloa. Unknown to me, somehow that fundamental, basic instinct for survival was keeping me moving.

As I stepped out of the vehicle, my right leg went limp, heavy, forcing me to lean against the vehicle for a couple of minutes to gather my strength. I hobbled towards the entrance, dragging my leg then climbed the stairs slowly using the handrails for balance. I shuffled into the office visibly relaxing as I made it to my seat and desk, relieved to be away from the pressures of lengthy driving. My work colleagues looked concerned as I limped around the office but I shrugged off the incapacity, determined to maintain at least a façade of bravado. I did manage to limp to the kitchen, prepare a pot of freshly brewed coffee, which placated the work mates, at least for a while. As it turns out, drinking strong fresh coffee was in fact probably not a very smart idea.

The morning passed very slowly. Work became an effort but as long as I was sitting, I felt better, fumbled through, remaining unusually quiet in the hope that my work mates would think I was deep in concentration. At lunchtime I went to the local supermarket for a sandwich. Alarmingly, after nearly six hours there was not any noticeable difference in my right leg, if anything the weakness was increasing, the capacity for walking diminishing hourly. Anxiety over my leg was escalating but what concerned me even more was the sudden realisation that I was experiencing extreme difficulty using my right hand. Shaking uncontrollably my hand was beginning to feel like a clumsy lump of lead, over which I had little control. In fact I was rapidly losing the entire control of my right hand, the fingers seeming to twist towards a claw like shape. It seemed as though the messages from the brain were simply not being delivered, impairing my physical control, mental concentration and understanding of what was actually going on around me. I sensed something awful was happening but could not understand what it was. I tried to remain calm although whatever was going on was leaving me very confused. It wasn't a case of paranoia but I did imagine that all focus of attention was upon me as I stood in the checkout queue, not fully convinced that I was actually coherent. I knew that I was speaking but not really sure of what I was saying. I imagined that the people in the queue beside me, looking at me probably thought that I was drunk or high on some drugs. Mind you even though it was lunchtime that probably would not have been an unusual sight in Alloa anyway.

There was a distinct feeling of being detached, my head a foggy vacant shell with a strange eerie silence within it. Confusion flooded through me, I neither knew nor understood what was happening and consequently was unable to fight back. I seriously believed for a short moment in time that madness was only an instant away. Desperately weak, confused, befuddled, I left the supermarket as quickly as I could shuffle, relieved to be away from prying eyes. But as I limped to the vehicle, I was fully aware that by now I was losing control, the fogginess inside my head growing worse, my sense of balance decreasing. I returned to the office but it was abundantly apparent that by now something very serious was happening. Whatever the problem, it was slowly killing off my thought process and capability for logical reasoning. For a brief moment a horrible sense of dread crashed through me – I really was frightened! What I did not know was that there was a time bomb ticking away inside my head. Ready to go off at any minute.

By mid afternoon, the weakness was increasing quite dramatically. As the day wore on I was finding it extremely difficult to use my calculator. Each time I left clicked my computer mouse, my other fingers would twitch involuntarily and hit the right-hand mouse key at the same time. The nerve ends were dying, I was losing control of my fingers, rapidly. As much as I tried to concentrate, co-ordination between brain and fingers became almost impossible. I struggled outside for some air. As I returned to the building, the receptionist, noticing my limp asked if I was

OK. I shrugged off the real answer, dismissing the lameness as a pulled muscle. She then advised me that there was a physiotherapist based in the building and it might be an idea to find out if she was available. Instead of climbing the stairs again, I took the lift to search out the physiotherapist's office. As it turned out, it was her day off or she was away from the office that afternoon. Whatever reason was unimportant. As it turns out had she been in attendance that day, I would probably have been immediately whisked off to the nearest hospital.

The afternoon passed slowly, very slowly. I became increasingly lost as my concentration faded away. Somehow, I struggled through the rest of the afternoon, fumbled my way through my work, hopefully concealing my limitations and ineptitude from my work mates. Just before five, I breathed a sigh of relief and set off for the car park. Instinctively I knew that it was unlikely that I would be back at work the next day. Hobbling down the stairs, clinging desperately to the handrails with my good left hand to steady myself, I could only drag my right foot in a shambled walk. I hauled myself into the Land Rover then sat, exhausted for a few minutes, trying to gather my thoughts, push some semblance of order into my increasingly befuddled brain. I forced myself to think hard, knowing full well that by now I was in a very worried state of mind, physical strength ebbing fast, mental alertness diminishing, desperate to get home but wasn't quite clear as to whether I could actually drive that distance. A feeling that I was close to blacking out washed through me but everything inside me urged me to get home, back to my own space and security. Whether I could do that without passing out was at that juncture, debatable. There was nothing in my head that could have argued the rights and wrongs of responsibility but a sudden surge of enthusiasm kick started the adrenalin. Maybe the fresh strong coffee had left just enough caffeine in my system to keep me alert, as decidedly low as that was. So I worked out an adrenalin-crazed plan or perhaps it was just crazed. Who knows? But the journey was broken into portions, the end of which I set as targets. Now what I was reasoning may not seem logical today but then, inside my bewildered mind it seemed to me quite sensible. I knew I was ill but didn't know what with. I also suspected that hospital might just not be too far away.

Therefore if I broke the journey into stages within the simple premise that if I had to give up at any point, at least I was closer to home. So it was from the office to the A907 roundabout; then along the A977 to the Kinross Junction; M90 past Perth then the A90 to Dundee. For most of the way it would be along comparatively straightforward driving conditions, motorways, dual carriageways. I set off slowly. There was no choice. I was simply not up to demanding conditions. Truth be known, I was probably not fit to be driving – full stop! I had no clear concept of time but gradually, the distances passed. As I reached the individual targets I relaxed ever so slightly although at one stage lost all sensation as to where I was actually heading. As the drive wore on, holding my right foot to the accelerator became a massive task, causing my speed to fluctuate. I made no attempt to overtake but instead stuck to the inside lane of the motorway or dual carriageway and tried to maintain a steady speed in which each mile was getting me that little bit closer to home.

Eventually, the high-rise buildings in the west end of Dundee came into view. But rather than being a welcome sight, alarm suddenly flashed through me as the awareness that I had at least eight busy roundabouts to negotiate before I could get back onto the comparatively straight forward Dundee to Aberdeen dual carriageway. Approaching the first junction at the start of the Kingsway, I realised that I could not feel the brake pedal under my foot. There was no sensation. I panicked again......! I'm going to crash. But I didn't. My right hand, progressively weakening, hung on to the steering wheel as my left hand and foot crashed down through the gears, slowing the vehicle, something that I could sense, rather than actually feel. With all the willpower I could muster, I started talking to myself giving out clear instructions or at least I think I did. For all intents I may well have been totally incoherent, garbling. But whatever! It worked. I let my brain or what was left of it control the situation. Now press with your foot . . . slowly . . . yes. I could feel the vehicle slowing, coming to a stop at the white lines or with sufficient room from the car in front. My brain seemed to have become some sort of a remote guidance unit delivering detached instructions. If I had been confused before, by now I think that I was as close as I have ever been to being completely barking mad. Now change gear, get into the inside lane and stay there. Good! Well Done! With each instruction, I acknowledged. Thank You! That short section of journey seemed interminable. Somehow, with a combination of hands, feet, rapidly diminishing brainpower I managed to clear the Kingsway. As the open section of the A90 was reached, I almost cried with relief. Strangely though, what seemed like overwhelming demands to me at that point actually appeared to clear my head momentarily. Perhaps, the fear, apprehension had again kicked in enough adrenalin to overcome the confusion. I do not know. There was no sense of time, nor did I care, but knew there were twenty-seven miles to go. Less than an hour later, I stumbled into the house, physically and mentally fatigued, completely drained.

Exhausted, I went to bed early after taking the obligatory aspirin. I was still convinced that I was suffering from some sort of muscle freeze or horrible flu bug but because I had made it home the immediate tension of the past two hours had disappeared. I actually slept well that night simply because by now, unknown to me my body was fighting off some apparent major damage, badly needed some very serious rest. It would however be a further twenty-four hours before I discovered just how severe the trauma was.

The next morning, I started off with my usual routine at just after five in the morning. Despite the worsening lack of feeling in my right arm and leg still being blatantly obvious I managed to get dressed. By now I was limping quite badly. The morning cup of day took great difficulty to make. The right hand was desperately weak, the limp profoundly worsened. With Tig beside me I set off on what should have been a brisk walk with the dog. I managed to get about a hundred metres from the house before I let Tig off to run around the undergrowth. From then on I lasted about fifty metres more before conceding defeat. After such a short distance I struggled desperately to get home, dragging a useless leg and foot along the ground. My sense of focus had gone, my mind by now totally confused, my head an empty shell. It felt as if some drunken stupor had taken over my body. Real fear and panic was setting in. I could just make out the strobe light on Tig's collar as he scampered about in the undergrowth but I needed him beside me. I knew that he would get me home. He became my priority, a focus for my concentration. If anything was about to happen to me I wanted to make sure that my faithful Springer would be safe? Slowly, we shuffled the short distance back to the house. There was little co-ordination between my brain and right hand as I attempted to slide the key into the lock in the side door of the house but found it impossible. My hand was weak, shaking, bouncing all over the place. Try as I might, I could not focus on the lock. I could see the lock, see my hand but getting the two to come together was impossible. Eventually, I succeeded in using my left hand then in a daze stumbled upstairs and into the bedroom. My wife Rose looked puzzled, then concerned as I limped into the room.

"My leg is useless," almost sobbing.

I lay down and stayed there. There was no hesitation on her part. As soon as the surgery opened Rose called to make an emergency appointment. She returned a few minutes later to let me know that I had a doctor's appointment in thirty minutes. In that time, I managed to get to the shower room then suddenly harsh reality brought me crashing down. As I tried to shave, I realised that I had no control over my right hand, none whatsoever, the blade simply stuck against my face. But determined to freshen up, I struggled slowly using my left hand instead. It was impossible to use my right hand even to squeeze toothpaste onto the brush. Instead I had to use my right elbow to hold down the brush whilst my left hand squeezed the paste on to it. Incapacitation overtook me in the shower, but somehow again managed to use my left hand to wash and shampoo. Panicking even more I realised I couldn't wash myself properly. The sobs eventually turned to a crazed stupid giggle when I was confronted with the sudden realisation that I couldn't even manage to wipe my own rear end. That strangely enough brought be back to earth with a sharp jolt. In a sense it was funny. But inside my head there was just confusion, no sense of clarity. It was a distressing situation for anyone. As a test, if you are right handed tie your arm to your side then try using your left for every daily function. That is what it felt like.

The medical appointment was brief and to the point. The doctor did not take any length of time over her diagnosis. My blood pressure was at a more than dangerously high level. In fact it was probably high enough to have killed someone off. The doctor scribbled out some notes, hastily wrote an introductory letter to the hospital admissions then instructed me to get there as fast as possible. Within twenty minutes of shuffling into the surgery, I was back home, a few items hastily thrown into a bag then I was off to the admissions ward of Ninewells Hospital in Dundee. But perplexingly as Rose drove along the busy roads that morning I actually started to relax. A few hours later a multitude of preliminary tests had been carried out. Firstly I was questioned, examined, blood samples taken, urine samples tested, my chest x-rayed. For a while as I sat in the waiting room, I quite firmly believed that I would be given a couple of pills and sent home. That is certainly what I was hoping for. But that didn't happen. A short time later a porter arrived with a wheelchair to take me to the admissions ward and a bed for the night. Soon after, the diagnosis was confirmed. I had joined the ranks of the victims of a horrible illness where the recovery rate can be as terrifyingly low as only 10 percent. I had suffered a stroke.

For me there was no going home that night or for a few after that. Instead I was admitted to a holding ward where most of the patients around me were heart attack victims. As I sat on the bed looking around me I did not believe that my being there held the same priority as those seriously ill people. There was no realisation of what was wrong with me nor did I understand exactly what had happened. I wanted out as fast as I could but that wasn't going to happen for a while either. For the first night sleep was constantly disrupted as my metabolism was monitored every hour for the first 24 hours.

I had already gained an unenviable reputation as being the man with the impressively high blood pressure although I didn't actually feel any worse for that. My sole concern was to get a decent night's sleep but that along with the other aspirations of a couple of pills and rapid discharge home wasn't going to happen either. The nurse kindly pulled the curtains around my bed to try to give me some semblance of privacy; block out some of the bright lights but the activity in the ward was ceaseless. This made it difficult to sleep in between the ritual awakening every hour on the hour. But gradually morning came and with it breakfast. I was famished. Under the misconception that I would be going home that afternoon I asked if I could shower and shave. The nurses were impressed. Limited in movement the morning ablutions took some time though. Then for the rest of the day life became a ritual of being trundled from one location to another where I was subjected to test after test. My body was x-rayed, my head scanned by CRT.

Rose arrived mid afternoon. I was more than pleased to see her but soon after a porter arrived with a wheelchair then trundled me off to the cardio-vascular unit where for a short period I lay helpless but intrigued as the machine recorded in perfect detail the flow of blood through my neck into my brain in glorious technicolour. Some time later, the porter returned me to the ward where my wife was waiting. We chatted for a while but I sensed she was holding something back from me. Not long after, the same porter arrived with the wheelchair, a staff nurse by his side. Relieved, I assumed it was time to be going home. But first I needed my clothes.

"They are keeping you in over the weekend," explained Rose. "You're being transferred to the Acute Stroke Unit."

"Oh no they are not," was my immediate reply. I was going home and that was the end of it.

"You're not well enough and you have to stay in for more tests on Monday", she reasoned.

"I'll come back on Monday then," I argued back.

The porter was sent away. The Staff Nurse sighed then disappeared. A short time later the Staff Nurse returned with the Consultant from the Acute Stroke Unit. The doctor was kind. She explained that the scans confirmed that I had suffered a stroke and really needed to be kept in hospital for a few more days where immediate care was available. In addition, there were a series of blood tests that needed to be carried out and as it was Friday these would have to be done after a fasting on Monday morning. I argued in a reasonable manner that I didn't have to walk upstairs in the house, we had a bedroom, shower and toilet downstairs and that I would be OK. I could also come back first thing in Monday morning. In all honesty, with the exception of being a bit paralysed, brain damaged and having high blood pressure, the latter which was thankfully, gradually diminishing, I felt fine. This all fell on deaf ears. I was rapidly coming to the conclusion that my wife and the doctor had conspired to keep me in. Then the doctor pulled her final punch.

"Stand up, please," she requested

I managed to stand – just.

"Now what I want you to do is to close your eyes, then with the first finger of your right hand, touch your nose." Demonstrating in the process.

I wobbled but managed to balance, closed my eyes then aiming for my nose with my finger, managed to miss my head completely. I tried again, and again! But however hard I tried; I simply could not touch my nose, my finger skimming the side of my face instead. Symptomatic of stroke victims my hand had gone into the characteristic claw shape.

"Mmmmmm," said the Doctor. Moving a few steps away from the bed into the ward.

"Sh*t", Then to myself, "I'm going to lose this."

"Walk towards me now please," the Doctor requested.

I tried. Honestly I did! Going home hinged on it. But I simply could not do it. My foot collapsed, I staggered then looked up at the Doctor.

"OK, you win," and smiled. Sheepishly!

The Doctor nodded and smiled. The porter returned smiling. The Staff Nurse smiled. Rose looked visibly relieved. Within minutes I was sitting on a bed near the window of a six-bed pod in Ward 4, the Acute Stroke Unit. The minute I sat on the bed, looked around me, I hated the place but I was close to a window and gazed longingly out at the trees and countryside. Unfortunately for me the temporary location comprised of women, making me even more uncomfortable, grumpier than I already was. Even worse the elderly lady in the next bed had an embarrassing habit of kicking off her bedclothes, throwing her legs in the air. I was mortified. The evening meal was eaten in a despondent sulky silence, not enjoying the food or the immediate company. My suggestion to the duty nurse that it would have taken three sheets tied together to enable me to abseil out of the ward window to freedom must have triggered more concern than I originally thought. A few moments later, I was told that I would be moving through to the next pod, which comprised of all men. Initially, I resisted, happy to be rebellious, if nothing else to be close to the window but the staff had the upper hand. Soon after I was in the next pod, the bed in a strategic position that could be seen from the ward desk. But I could not relax. Around me there were some pretty disturbing sights of very ill people, some unable to walk, eat, drink or communicate. Looking around the ward it was plain to see the hopelessness that surrounded some of the patients, the physical degeneration, the blank stares of eyes that had long since given up the fight. There were the occasional groans as someone turned or shifted in their beds, secured by guardrails. The place was packed full of medical machines that threw out a steady noisy thrum as high protein food was forced into the patients stomachs by tube. It was a very sad place to be. Then as night gradually fell and the shadows cast by a sinking sun filtered through the large window, my body went through the aftershock and as can happen the second trauma when it came, struck with a vengeance!

§

A stroke is when an area of the brain is deprived of its blood supply - usually because of a blockage or burst blood vessel - for long enough to cause vital brain tissue to die. It's essentially the same as what happens in the arteries leading to the heart when someone has a heart attack, which is why a stroke is now often described as a 'brain attack'. There are two types of stroke, 90% of which are **ischaemic** strokes, caused by a blockage in an artery, which affects blood flow to, or within, the brain. An ischaemic stroke can also be called a **Transient Ischaemic Attack or TIA**, if it happens for less than 24 hours. TIAs are an important warning sign that all is not well with the blood supply to the brain. The risk of suffering a complete stroke within the first month after a TIA may be as high as 20 per cent, with the risk being even greater in the first few hours or days following a TIA.

The other 10% are haemorrhagic strokes, also called brain haemorrhages where there is a bleed in the brain. There are also events, which might be called strokes or might be called cerebrovascular accidents, which have similar results to strokes. An example of this would be an aneurysm in the brain. This is a swelling of an artery, which balloons outwards and can damage or destroy brain cells as it does so. Traditionally it has been said that if symptoms last less than 24 hours it's a TIA, but when symptoms persist for more than 24 hours then a stroke has occurred. But with more powerful and sophisticated brain-scanning techniques, it has become possible to show that permanent damage (the real hallmark of a stroke) can usually be detected when symptoms last more than an hour or so. The causes are many, ranging from diseased arteries - blockage of the arteries is usually the result of arteriosclerosis - furring and narrowing of the artery walls with a mixture of cholesterol and other debris. An aneurysm - a weakened spot on an artery wall causes it to stretch. The vessel wall may become so thin it bursts, causing bleeding into the brain (haemor-rhagic stroke). Or atrial fibrillation - this kind of irregular heartbeat (arrhythmia) can cause a blood clot to form in the heart, which then travels to the brain.

Whatever the causes or severity of the aftermath, this is a dangerous debilitating disease that discriminates against non-one. The term stroke is apt because symptoms gener-ally appear suddenly and without warning - 'at a stroke'. If a stroke is suspected, it is vital to get medical help quickly – FAST! The sooner treatment is given, the less damage there is likely to be to the brain tissue, the better the odds of a good recovery. In the UK stroke is the third most common cause of death. It is also the single most common cause of severe disability. More than 250,000 people in this country live with disabilities caused by stroke. Every year over a 130,000 people in the UK have a stroke of vary levels of severity, different degrees of disability. Statistically that is one person every five minutes. Most people affected by stroke are over sixty-five years of age but anyone can have a stroke, including children and even babies. Around a thousand people under thirty-five years of age have a stroke every year. Almost one in four men and one in five women aged forty-five can expect to suffer stroke if they live to be eighty-five. More than three times as many women die from stroke than breast cancer in the UK. But strangely there are unacceptable inadequacies in stroke care and research. For every £50 spent on cancer research and £20 on heart research, only a £1 is spent on stroke research. It is without doubt a terrible illness with catastrophic aftermath. And it discriminates against no one.

§

So there it was. I had suffered a stroke. My body was lying on a hospital bed within a pod of the Acute Stroke Unit in Dundee's Ninewells Hospital. My soul was else-where. For all purposes I was now somewhere inside the heavenly void, the final path, transition from mortality to death. But, as I concentrated on the light, it grew slowly yet steadily in brightness and size to form a bright glowing circle, the dimensions of which to me were immeasurable. Bright rainbow patterned rays of multi-coloured light shone all around, forcing back the merciless darkness. There was no conscience decision on my part to either move towards the light or away from it. I stood transfixed, yet concen-trated all my effort on that brightening circle. The light grew brighter. Peace surrounded me and I thought of nothing else but the ring of light that seemed to be inviting me towards it. Confusion disappeared to be replaced with an inner sense of tranquillity and affection that I do not think I had ever felt before. I let the peace and calmness wash over me. And the light grew stronger. Any feeling of sadness disappeared fast. And the circle of light grew larger.

Shafts of bright rainbow patterns appeared, probing outwards. I quickly glanced around me, took in the darkness, the mist with the eerie flickering shapes and shadowy beings and chose the light. And the light grew brighter. I focussed back at the shimmering circle of light that guarded what appeared to be an entrance, a passageway perhaps, but still could not move towards it.

As I strained harder into the light I saw something, a ghostly creature, a being of light materialising from the brightness, rushing straight toward me. It was a big, gleaming, splendid horse that emerged from the light, racing in my direction. Fascinated I stood my ground; some hidden sense told me there was nothing to fear. The equine spectre came nearer, slowed then came to a standstill right alongside me. He stood perfectly still staring straight ahead. The horse did not look at me but I could feel the heat from his body, felt the warm air as it blew from his nostrils. Instinctively, I knew that somehow I had to get onto that horse and I would be safe, free from the darkness. As I reached towards the horse, I was suddenly and overwhelmingly subsumed with a bursting passion for life. A shock went though my body as my hand touched the horses flank. Strength powered through me. The paralysis hadn't gone but I was no longer aware of the limitations. Some strange unknown quirk of destiny was moulding my direction and I could feel myself almost sobbing with elation as I stretched up for the mane, awkwardly heaved myself up. The horse remained steady throughout as I swung my right leg into place. As the mount started to walk slowly towards the darkness ahead, I felt calm, very much at peace but an overriding sense of excitement coursed through me. From Herd and The Underworld:

"Out of the land of shadows and darkness"
"You are returning with us, the morning light"

Without any bidding, the horse started to walk, then to trot, almost immediately the momentum grew, the pace increased. As it did so, I sat up straight and looked clearly ahead, my head held high. The darkness was disappearing to be replaced with great shafts of bright rainbow patterns that broke all around me. I laughed aloud. The gait increased. Then the faster we rode the faster the darkness diminished, retreating into the background. Ahead of me I was no longer staring into blackness. The shadows were receding; the light intensified cascading behind me, around me. Soon I was riding through a bright world with clear blue skies, sunlight bathing my face, rainbow colours exploding everywhere around me. I felt totally bonded, at oneness with the horse.

The faster we rode the louder I laughed, a new zest for life crashing through my body. Everywhere was an amazing assortment of colour. As brightness surrounded me the gloominess, the mist disappeared. The shadowy eerie shapes and figures no longer existed, they were gone somewhere behind me, destroyed in the brightness. I did not look back, just concentrated on what was ahead. And ahead were brightness, peace, calmness, tranquillity and a new future. I had touched the void but now I was out of the darkness. Somehow, for some reason, fate had stepped in, allowed me to return. Without any real conscious thought I was very, very aware that something extraordinary had irrevocably just shaped my destiny.

Keeping the Faith

"Strong is the faith that keeps me alive. Secure in the knowledge that I will survive."

THE next morning I woke remarkably refreshed. A strange sense of spiritual well being, tranquility and profound affection stayed with me. In a certain respect I felt immortal, sensing a glow, an aura that not only hung over me but was inside me. I firmly believed that I had risen above a plane transcending the earthly world but was now firmly back to reality. Then again maybe not! I also felt more than a little confused about the entire experience, but temporarily shrugged this off because for the time being the dream, mental picture, whatever it might have been, was relegated to second position in the pecking order of physical and mental recovery. Constantly exhausted I drifted into the deep sleep of recovery whenever I could but still the experience of the tunnel, the encounter with the ghostly horse stayed to continually haunt me.

When I eventually left Ninewells Hospital, pushed through the wards in a wheel chair by the same friendly porter, it was as a changed person. Physically I remained weak, arm and leg still semi-paralysed, a part of the brain damaged apparently beyond repair. There were further issues; medical matters that apparently required deeper investigation and clarification. Those points of concern included arteriosclerosis, borderline diabetes, and an enlarged heart. None of those sounded particularly appealing or an immediate source of amusement; each had its own drawbacks, limitations. As it transpired there was nothing to worry about as future tests showed. In general, I felt marvellous, subsumed by a new spiritual sense of peace and tranquillity, a belief that I was close to being immortal. I was happy to be home, happy to be alive. I accepted that whatever it would take to get back to as normal a life as possible was achievable.

It would have been easy, so easy just to give up, to slip away into a nether world like the lost souls in the mistiness. Maybe, just maybe if that strange almost paranormal experience had not occurred, I might possibly have joined the ranks of the despondent, incapacitated lost victims. Stroke is a debilitating illness that doesn't just strike at physical characteristics but because of what has become known as a brain attack, stroke can undermine the victim's mental and psychological capacity or indeed mental ability to fight back. Instinctively I knew that the struggle for full recovery had to start energetically. Despite the aching fatigue, the mental turmoil and confusion I was certainly not going to give in or give up. Someone had once said that you always know those who are going to get better. They fight it. They do not let it win. Unfortunately, for most people that may well be easier said than done. But if there was one thing that I knew how to do well – that was to fight.

There were no real choices or alternatives, a new routine started, necessary to prevent me slipping into lazy ways or conceding defeat to the pervading weakness that could quite easily destroy my new zest for life and living. Each day I had to force myself to get out of bed then limp to the toilet for a shower and shave. Although I could not go anywhere nor was I capable of walking anything more than very short distances, I utilised my time as best I could. The morning ritual would include some light exercises with weights, then a lot of reading to help focus my mind and brain into recovery. Despite the damage to my right hand, I persevered with my writing even in Gaelic, until eventually within a few weeks I was able to again present a reasonable pass for my signature. Apart from a high weekly dosage of prescription drugs, which included statins and other clot-busting medicines, there was nothing in my nutritional regime that had to change because there was nothing really bad about the pre-stroke eating habits. My cholesterol level was way below average figures anyway, so there were no rigorous alterations to my food intake. But oddly, a crushing passion for green apples developed and at the same time my normal love of fish became a major addiction. Brain food perhaps!

But the insidious exhaustion stayed on. Although a recognised phenomenon, the reason for fatigue is not fully understood. Sleep disturbance may be caused by damage to areas of the brain controlling the body's sleep-wake cycle. For me I simply believed that it was nature's way of helping a damaged body to repair. Just as it seemed that in some small way, each new dawn was bringing about a slow recovery or improved competence the roller coaster of emotional turmoil finally started to take its toll. Slowly, but progressively the aftermath, the side effects of stroke crept into my well-being. Gradually, the marvellous feeling of euphoria started to diminish as the negative aspects and emotional upheaval fought to gain control. For the first time I became aware of cognitive difficulties including problems associated with damage to areas of the brain. My mental processes such as thinking clearly and logically, paying attention, memory and decision making seemed to be in disarray. As for forward planning, I was lost. Behaviourally, I sensed that further changes had taken place. My reactions became slower, organisational capability deteriorated. As I experienced difficulties in adjusting to these changes, I became more confused, irritated and frustrated. What surprised me even more was the realisation that suddenly just as my writing was improving, dyslexia became a harsh symptomatic reality.

Disoriented, confused, frantically struggling to retain my mental balance and credibility, once more I became locked in a battle for survival. What in fact was actually happening was the transition from one phase of the aftermath and recovery to the next. Typically the spontaneous recovery, the feeling of euphoria when lost abilities are regained begins to taper off. This was a frustrating time as suddenly I became aware of my own limitations, brutally conscious of the fact that invincibility is nothing more than an illusion, a figment of the imagination, immortality nothing more than a dream. There also came the point where frustration, anger, bitterness and general feelings of despondency became acutely manifest. And at times those spilled over into bouts of rage or temper tantrums more characteristic of an adolescent than a grown man.

Somewhere amongst the mass of information thrust upon me, I had read that stroke victims, survivors should grieve for their loss. Perhaps because a bit of the brain has died there is some mileage in mourning for a lost life or a part of it. Who knows? Maybe just for a short while that is exactly what I did. I felt sorry for myself, worried about what the future might hold, concerned for the limitations thrust upon me, disgusted and bitter that this had happened to me. The thought that I might remain permanently paralysed, damaged, crippled worried me considerably. Automatically banned from driving, trapped inside for nearly a month, I was close to falling into a state of helplessness where I could not even take my dog out for a walk. Of course there was always the self-help groups, or the reams of documented "survivors" stories on the Internet to identify with. There was the overriding temptation to research stroke, to find out more about the illness, the causes, the reasons why someone reasonably fit, healthy and active can be struck down just as easily as the comparatively unhealthy or ailing. But I had no intention in wallowing in the company of self-pity, nor did the endless tales of how stroke had affected the lives of others hold any interest for me. What I wanted to learn about was recovery, how to beat the monster, overcome what had become a very real enemy. In fact I likened the whole concept of accepting life as a victim or survivor as quite alien, definitely defeatist, most definitely not for me. Dwelling on an illness or its imposed limitations as a member of some self help group or club was completely opposed to my independent nature anyway. It might seem an odd comparison but there did seem to be a degree of similarity with the Stockholm syndrome. The apparent type of behaviour characterised by the haste to seek identification with the illness or others affected by association or de-individuation struck me as a very close resemblance to the psychology of the hostage scenario that spawned the term.

The incident in the Swedish capital that led to the term Stockholm syndrome had nothing to do with politics or terrorism. It was a bank robbery, pure and simple that took place at the Kreditbanken in Norrmalmstorg, Stockholm. What made it unique was the psychoanalytical research carried out afterwards as a result of the hostage's behaviour, in particular dependency. In cases where Stockholm syndrome has occurred, the captive is in a situation where the captor has stripped nearly all forms of independence and gained control of the victim's life, giving life by simply not taking it. The Austrian psychologist L. Mann claims that

the syndrome tends to develop in three stages. Firstly the
initial shock and panic is often followed by apathy and
despair. Secondly there is ambivalence and emotional
dependency, then finally acceptance of the scenario. Of
course it is a lot more complex than that but nevertheless
there is an odd comparision with the stages of stroke and
indeed probably a lot of other illnesses. Around a third of
strokes are fatal. Survivors are grateful because life was not
taken away. Assistance is then needed to overcome the
despondency and despair that can follow the initial shock
and panic and assistance inevitably means dependency.
Secondly there is the emotional turmoil, the characteristic
mood swings, anxiety attacks or depression. Those symptoms in turn require further assistance, treatment, and
medication. Very soon that assistance can manifest itself in
greater dependency and ultimately loss of independence.
Eventually the monster wins and the stroke survivor
becomes the slave to circumstance. In consequence that is
why the associations, web sites, the self help groups and
the inappropriately named "clubs" thrive because ultimately the victim has accepted the illness as being the
master and can find solace in like-minded individuals.
Perhaps the association with the Stockholm syndrome as a
comparison is wildly inaccurate but there is a striking
similarity to the psychological aspects of the various stages
immediately following and in the aftermath of a stroke.
Whether any particular attention is paid to the requirements
for mental and psychological renovation seems vague. It is
surprising just how many people are prepared to dwell on
the illness, maintain the association rather than develop any
urgency in the need for recuperation. But dwelling on the
illness was definitely one option that I firmly shied away
from.

In the weeks that went past, perseverance was the tactic, recovery the strategy. I knew that apart from physiological limitations there were other changes that had occurred. Emotions seemed to have twisted and turned. Small things, pettiness or nastiness displayed by others were found to be deeply upsetting causing uncharacteristic sensitivity, whereas wider emotional issues were perfectly managed. Rehabilitation was a slow and frustrating progression. There were periods of time when it appeared that little progress had been made. That caused even more infuriation.

For a long time I was accompanied wherever I went by a string of bright lights that dangled just to the side and ahead of my right eye. That annoyed and frustrated me even further but it was a temporary problem, symptomatic of the aftermath of a brain trauma. Each day was a measured, calculated step. Literally! But I was fortunate. Rose encouraged, praised any progress, no matter how small it may have appeared, and constantly helped to motivate me to achieve long-term goals. Gradually the pronounced limp lessened, as muscular stength returned slowly. Embarrassingly though my right leg would occasionally, involuntarily kick out in spasms or my right hand would wobble as the nerve ends healed or messages from the brain started getting through. Repetitive weight training developed the co-ordination and strength in my arm and hand. It was a pleasure to be able to eat properly again without the food being catapulted over my shoulder or on to my legs. Physically the nerve ends began to receive the correct messages as the brain adapted, co-ordination improved. From a physiological perspective progress became more rapid as each week went by, the battle slowly, hesitantly but decisively being won.

But there is more to mending than just the rejuvenation of physical strength, strengthening muscles and nerve ends.

Someone who has had a stroke can often seem as though they have had a change in personality, or they can sometimes appear to act irrationally. This is due to the psychological and cognitive impact of a stroke. At times, I became angry or resentful; overwhelmed by bitterness, occasionally bouncing objects off walls in frustration, but the rehabilitation progressed. Recovery and rehabilitation from stroke present particular challenges. One day fit and well, the next moment disabled. The stroke survivor must come to terms with physical and emotional changes as well as significant new lifestyle adjustments - mobility, job, income, dependence, relationships - everything changes. It was a life changing experience and one that would be with me for life, in reality something that could be managed but never truly defeated. If the short term effects of stroke or the lingering longer term affects had left me ill equipped to deal with the rigours of normal life, the after effects of the near death experience placed me in a championship category all by myself.

And the image, dream or whatever it was continued to disturb me. I looked back to that night in the ward and tried hard to remember what had happened. Recollection was easy, the experience still vivid within my memory. As try as I might, I could not find any real significance in what I had seen or experienced. Had this really been a Near Death Experience (NDE)? If so, what did it all mean? Why a horse of all creatures? The more I thought of the notions, the more confused I became. Undeniably I had been brought up in a family where religion, Christianity still held sway. My parents owed their upbringing to the Free Church of Scotland on my Mother's side, on my Fathers - Presbyterianism. My maternal grandfather was also a lay preacher, a reader in the Free Church, a cousin an ordained Reverend in the Presbyterian; at one time Sundays held a place for bible study and worship only. From an early age I followed the background to their beliefs, indeed I was just touching sixteen years of age before my association with Sunday school, Bible Class and church attendance ceased altogether. There was no conscious effort at that time to move away from the church. As a teenager it just happened, peer pressure, other things in life took over.

But I would be the last to deny the existence of God, the principles of fundamentalist Christianity; my mind remains open, fearful of doubt – just in case, the icy tentacles of Calvinism never too far away from native Scots. With equal conviction, I found it easier to accept Jesus, the physical manifestation of a messiah or prophet more credible to a mind that tends to gravitate towards scientific thought. Consequently, I did not consider myself to be a religious or pious person. In fact many of the allegedly devout Christians I have met struck me by their abject, overt displays of hypocrisy and greed. These were the sorts of people that would unwittingly turn others away from a faith through their own selfishness. But despite this, the tunnel with its twisting mysterious shapes, the light and the encounter with the ghostly horse, the being of light suggested that maybe a degree of religious background, spiritualism existed or maybe something else could be associated with what might be interpreted as a life experience. That hypothesis continued to haunt me for many days, weeks and months thereafter.

No matter which way I tried to examine the experience, there never seemed to be a logical explanation. Perhaps, I reasoned that the dream or whatever it could be described as was in fact merely a figment of a tortured mind, the aftermath of brain damage. Or perhaps, the early stages of the medicines created some sort of hallucinatory effect to trigger some deep-rooted thought process or illusion somewhere inside my sub conscious. But whichever direction I turned to seeking guidance or reassurance, or an answer, it can be stated quite categorically that such a dream had neither occurred before nor at any time afterwards. It was indeed a one off experience. Accordingly, the spiritual aspect both scared and confused me. There were too many imponderables, too few clear answers. I struggled to comprehend the whys and wherefores, becoming more confused as time wore on but still the experience haunted me.

Whichever way you look at it, the concept of near death experiences is a difficult subject, depending on your point of view is either deeply objective or very subjective. The topic probably conjures up a number of different yet specific schools of thought; enthusiasm, scepticism or amused indifference being some of them. Some people grasp the concept eagerly, seeking some spiritual explanation or confirmation that an afterlife, a heavenly realm exists and that there is a process between death and the spirit world. It's a nice thought. Cynics denounce the idea as lacking in any real explanation or scientific proof, preferring instead to look at the sub conscious transmitting its final signals as the brain dies. Or maybe somehow the intervention of chemicals or medical drugs triggers a process as death approaches. One doctor from the University of New Mexico advanced the theory that a massive release of dimethyltryptamine from the pineal gland might be the cause of the near death experience phenomena. Others argue that the near death experience cannot be completely explained by physiological or psychological causes, and that consciousness can function independently of brain activity. But who really knows? As Omar Khayyam, the Persian scholar said in the Rubaiyat:

> *"Strange is it not that of the myriads who,*
> *Before us pass'd the door of darkness through*

Not one has returned to show us the road
Which to discover we must travel too."

There is plenty of material around, descriptions of people having had out of body experiences whilst close to death through severe illness or clinically dying on the operating theatre. It was not really a subject that I had paid much attention to. In consequence I had no worthwhile concept or knowledge whatsoever of anyone experiencing the void. Therefore, it was probably inevitable that curiosity would eventually drive me to investigate further. What I found disturbed me. Based on various research projects, "scientific" investigations, psychological analysis and statistics, the information all seemed to lead to the same conclusions. It is an interesting hypothesis that will probably continue to provoke debate until the end of time. Whatever direction or theory people choose to follow, acceptance, rejection, complete indifference is really irrespective to me but it is highly likely that some people may find the following interpretation quite distressing.

Many near death accounts involve a description of travelling through a realm that is commonly known in NDE circles as - the void. Together with the earthbound realm, the void is known by many religious traditions as purgatory, hell or outer darkness. It is believed that after death some souls travel very quickly through the two lower realms – the earthbound realm and the void by means of the tunnel and on to a higher realm. Other souls, particularly those who have developed a strong addiction for an earthly desire that went beyond the physical and into the spiritual may enter the earthbound realm in a vain attempt to re-enter earth. However, many near death experiences involve souls entering the void immediately after death. From there the souls may enter the tunnel toward the light and the next heavenly realm. Other souls remain in the void for one reason or another until they are ready to leave.

Tradition suggests that the void is totally without love, light and everything. It is a realm of complete and profound darkness where nothing exists but the thought patterns of those in it. It is the perfect place for souls to contemplate their recent earthly experiences, examine their own mind and decide where they want to go next.

The void is not punishment. On the contrary it is the perfect place for all souls to see themselves. For some the void is a beautiful and heavenly experience because in the absence of all else they are able to perfectly see the love and light they have cultivated within themselves. For others it is a terrifying, horrible hell because in the absence of everything they are able to perfectly see the lack of love and light that they have cultivated within themselves. For this reason the void is more than a place for reflection or to purge themselves from every illusion – it is a place of purification.

Interpretation would suggest that for some the time spent in the void might be instantaneous. For others it may seem like eternity. This is because the only way to escape the void is to choose between the light and darkness. For those who refuse the light or have spent a lifetime ignoring it, the time spent in the void may seem endless before they reach the point that they desire the light of love. The problem for many is that they prefer, for one reason or another, darkness to light.

The outer edges of the realm have been described as shadowy, greyish and foggy. But there are various degrees of darkness in this realm. It is darker, denser at the centre than at the outer fringes. The closer to the centre the darker and more painful is the solitude. The nearer to the outer edges, the more interaction there is with others in the realm.

That interaction is not necessarily a very pleasant experience. In the void the darkest of human nature can be found if you desire to seek it. It is a region of tormented hate filled souls, suicides, cruel and evil people, their faces distorted by hatred, greed, malice or other defeating emotions, all of whom may remain in the realm for eons until they turn towards and accept the light. Some souls fill the void with an irrational and astonishing amount of pain and fear. People who have chosen to live corrupt or cruel lives and have turned their backs on the light of God find themselves in a state similar to groping in the dark and depressing fog. Wrapped up in their own cruel thinking, these souls wander around in a lost state until they of their own volition make an attempt to turn towards the light.

The nature of love and light is that it cannot be thrust upon anyone who does not want it. Choosing love and light over the darkness is the key to being freed from the void. The moment the choice is made the tunnel and light appear and the soul is drawn into the light. But the only love and light that exists in the void is the love that you bring in to it. For those whose life on earth has been filled with love and light, the passage may be instantaneous. For others it may seem like an era as indecision, lack of direction, or reflection determines the duration of stay. Other souls remain in the void for one reason or another until they are ready to leave it.

A darkness rules in the void but the void is a spiritual struggle between the darkness and light of the individual, a reflection of a fundamental sense of purity. Once light and love is chosen the soul's stay is ended. But some souls become trapped in the void for various reasons. Virtually any earthly desire that becomes so obsessive that it goes beyond the physical and extends into the spiritual has the ability to prevent people from realising the divine love and light within them. Escaping from the void is easy for some souls, extremely difficult for others. Then there are those who do not belong in the void because they have not gone past the end of their earthly physical life. For those unwilling to enter the light there may be only one choice and that is to return to earth. But beings of light exist in the void and are nearby and ready to help anyone in the void out of their predicament. All it takes is but a desire, a cry for help, no matter how large or small and they will be automatically rescued from the void, set free from the darkness. As they merge into one with the being of light they return with a new radiance burning inside them. For me that being of light just happened to be a horse and to say the least that was extremely puzzling.

Based on a wide range of research conducted by academics, doctors, and psychologists it would appear that by definition I had touched the void. From a plethora of information available for investigation the layers of darkness, the lost tormented souls unable to choose between darkness and light, the tunnel and the being of light all made a degree of sense. Understanding what happened or what had been seen is one thing, explanations or acceptance are completely separate subjects. For many people who have had a near death experience there is the overwhelming suggestion that they have been given a glimpse of life after death. No matter what the nature of the experience, it alters lives. If the stroke had dramatically altered my physiological capability and mental outlook on life, the encounter with the ghostly horse, the being of light and escape from the void brought about an entire paradigm shift.

The values that you get from a near death experience are not the ones needed to function in everyday life. There is no doubt that it was a profound emotional experience that left me a lot less materialistic and a lot more caring than I had ever been. In a sense there had been a radical turna-round, almost if I had become another person. Familiar codes of conduct lost relevance or disappeared altogether as what seemed to be unlimited avenues of interest took priority. To the prima facie observer it may well have seemed that I had actually become more aloof, un-respon-sive, even uncaring or un-loving.

But nothing could have been further from the truth. In fact those implied characteristics occasionally left me feeling quite upset and isolated. On the contrary to a wrongly perceived standoffish or isolated temperament, inside myself a deeper accepting nature, almost childlike naiveté existed. Not quite altruistic but definitely a lot less selfish with a much greater sense and awareness of inequalities or social injustice. Indeed I almost came to recognize myself as an immortal soul currently resident within material form, sojourning in the earth realm but thinking and dwelling in a much higher celestial plane. It was certainly not insanity. I assume that may well have been picked up on one of my routine health checks. Maybe not! Nevertheless, these are not exactly the characteristics or values needed to cope with the rigours of the materialistic, grasping, rude and greedy aspects of modern day life. However, as someone said, there is more to the human spirit than can be proven scientifically, and there is more to living than our sensory faculties define.

I am probably still unconvinced that I had witnessed the journey to heaven or stared eternity in the face but do accept with tenacity what happened. What I saw and subsequently felt was very real. The horse? Of all creatures why a horse appearing to lead me out of the tunnel, out of the darkness and mist – back into the light?

Up until that point, my association with horses was minimal, having only ever ridden three times over a period of the preceding ten years. Even then I wasn't particularly enamoured with the creatures, the trekking over the hills was at the behest of my wife and daughters to join them. Certainly in one particular occasion, the great brute of a creature that I was given seemed to have a sole purpose in life, its prime directive being to dispense me from his back at any opportunity. If it had fire and smoke breathing from its nostrils and a bolt through its neck, the description may have been more appropriate. To say that I enjoyed the two-hour excursion across the mountains in Arran soaked through in the heaving rain; miserable grey low cloud would be a gross misrepresentation of fact. Tightly, I held on to the reins, kept my boots firmly in the stirrups and sat clinging on for dear life. The additional fact that I had severe difficulty in sitting down without a pillow under my aching backside for about three days afterwards did nothing to suggest that I had a future as a rider. Rose and the girls thought the entire painful process I went through in the aftermath of what was really a gentle pony trek to be hilarious. I did not particularly empathize with their humour. Sympathy seemed to be non-existent!

Being the butt, if you pardon the pun, of their hilarity and amusement didn't really appeal to my fragility. In fact at that point in time, I would have been perfectly happy never to see another equine as long as I lived. If riding meant being unable to walk properly for days on end or necessitated an ample layer of quilted padding to protect my damaged rear end – forget it! To put it simply - I just did not enjoy the experience. At that juncture I probably had about as much understanding, oneness or affection with a horse as I would have playing football with a live grenade that had a perilously loose pin.

But there it was, a tunnel, the being of light - a ghostly horse, acceptance of the light then freedom from the darkness and misty shadows, the escape on horseback. As far as I was concerned there was no explanation for either. Perhaps there is? Perhaps a psychologist could find some deep-seated reason for the manifestation of the horse. I certainly could not but unquestionably this left me very puzzled and confused, the quest for a logical conclusion too difficult. Any cognitive thought process failed to discover a sensible outcome that could be accepted in a practical manner. The more I tried to debate the subject within my own perspective, the more perplexed or mystified I became.

In legends told throughout the Far East, central Asia, Europe, and the Middle East, horses were considered mediums between the Spirit and Material Worlds. Certain Celtic tribes used a white mare as an oracle. Arabic tales exalted the horse's sixth sense. Horses were also perceived as carrying riders between the seen and unseen realms or leading people to some form of lost knowledge. Modern Yakut shamans would not dream of visiting the *Otherworld* without the aid of their horses.

Exalted in legend, horses are considered to be spirit guides on a journey to discover our inner selves, encouraging us to 'be in the moment'. The size of such an animal alone inspires a heightened state of awareness. When we engage with the horse with no agenda but to enter into the circle of life and just 'be', we enter a gateway that brings us more fully into the present moment and moves us into alignment with life. We place ourselves in the sacred realm of the natural world, open the way for experience, reflections and dialogue and then stand aside and allow the process to happen.

Horses play a substantial role in the spiritual beliefs of many cultures such as Shamanism where they represent powerful spirit guides. Within such a background the spirit guide chooses the person, not the other way around. It is also believed that the spirit guide appears at a fork in the road of life. When a decision is made to follow a certain path in life, the spirit is there to serve as a guide along the way. It represents a path that may take months or years to complete, a friendly travelling companion if the path is right. If you become lost along the way, the spirit guide is there to help lead the way back.

This guide seemingly remains at your side until the current cycle in your life has changed or may remain a part of you throughout life's journey and reflects your inner-spiritual self. Usually a spirit guide does not move away or disappear but remains an integral part of your life, however, there are instances when a particular spirit guide is no longer needed and is replaced with a new one. Apparently, its powers are always there for you and serve as a constant reminder of your inner powers and oneness with nature.

The horse is indeed a noble and powerful animal. For centuries it has inspired writers, artists and poets. Since time immemorial man has enjoyed a special relationship with the horse. Humans, mankind have benefited from the horses strength and loyalty and in return we have bestowed on him a status, which is perhaps above that of all other creatures. As Duncan Ronald said in his wonderful poem:

> *"Where in this wide world can man find*
> *nobility without pride?*
> *Friendship without envy, beauty without vanity,*
> *Here where grace is laced with muscle*
> *And strength by gentleness confined"*

As a dream symbol it can represent a wide range of positive thoughts and ideas about oneself or others. At times, they can also be considered messengers, relaying information from the unconscious to the conscious, from the spiritual to the physical. To see a horse in your dream,

symbolizes strength, power, and endurance. It also represents a strong, physical energy, movement or a new adventure, whether it is physical or spiritual. If the horse is white,
then it signifies purity, prosperity and good fortune. For
me two out of three of those did not really sound like too
bad a deal after all. I could have coped with that. But that
vision, the encounter with the ghostly horse - the being of
light and now the concept of spirit guides really did
continue to puzzle me, if for no other reason than the lack
of a satisfactory explanation or conclusive scientific answer.

Short-term effects disappear with time as any swelling
in the brain goes down and the damaged cells surrounding
the dead brain cells are repaired. Long-term effects are
caused by the death of brain tissue. They wont go away,
but they can often be modified with rehabilitation. Brain
cells that have died cannot start working again. However
areas of the brain affected by swelling caused by stroke may
recover as the swelling goes down. The brain is very
adaptive and with time can often find new ways to transmit
information (new neural pathways) to avoid the damaged
areas. But the brain needs encouraged, developing these
pathways in exactly the same way as learning a musical
instrument or in fact riding a horse (therapeutic riding) is
encouraging the development of co-ordination of the body.
I was quite keen to learn to play the saxophone, but knew
full well that it would be a very long time if ever that the
fingers of my right hand could function to the level of a
competent musician.

§

As the days passed into weeks, the weeks to months my
resolution to extract myself from physical weakness grew
stronger. I still believed, quite firmly that I might well be
on some specific purpose in a new life but had no idea of

what that was. The background to the stroke, its aftermath, the pathway to recovery or the semblance of a normal life had been examined in detail. I found what knowledge I needed to learn then turned my back on any disabilities, became hostile to any suggestion of invalidity and did my utmost to shy away from any association with other survivors. On a similar basis, I looked very closely at the experience of touching the void, learned what I could, and then reluctantly accepted with tenacity what I cannot change or logically challenge. Of course the encounter with the horse still puzzled me. I liked the idea of a spirit guide, especially a horse because the equine signifies freedom. For me freedom has always been sacrosanct. Maybe there was some greater significance? If there were it was beyond me. Just as I had accepted the background to the stroke, learned what I needed to know to get better then moved on, I accepted the realisation that it was now time to extricate myself from the confusion of the tunnel and the being of light. But there was one further thing that I felt had to be done, the final piece of exorcism to put the entire spooky episode of the stroke, near death experience, the void, beings of light and equine spirit guides well and truly behind me and move on.

Extraordinarily enough it came without any real semblance of conscious thought. One morning I woke up and decided on one thing. If the ghost had to be put to rest – finally – and really there was little choice in the decision that had to be made, fears, apathy, apprehension had to be confronted. Prepared to meet head-on those emotions, I was going to have to learn to ride a horse. If for no other reason, I genuinely wanted to experience what it would really be like to be at oneness with what later did become an association with wonderful, very special animals. More importantly if a horse did signify some specific purpose in my life then I was more than prepared to let it lead me on whatever journey may be in store. There were no aspirations for greatness, no future plans for competition, no desire to engage in ego boosting falsehoods - just learn to ride properly or as best I could, or in the worst case scenario if fate decided otherwise, then not at all. It was simple, spontaneous and "uncomplicated". That is exactly how it happened.

Boots and Saddles

"Take life on earth to the second birth".

A SHORT while later I turned up at a riding centre, slightly nervous, not really sure what to expect, yet determined to see the whole thing through, irrespective of how long it might take. In a matter of months I had climbed out of a wheelchair and now with more than just a shade of trepidation was about to climb on to the back of what looked like a very large scary horse. Even to the bravest person, being perched high atop a large animal can quite easily induce a sense of vulnerability. It wasn't really – initially it just seemed that way. But I was fortunate because although I was about to be placed in the hands of a slightly formidable looking lady with years of physiological and equestrian experience her manner dissolved any negative thoughts of doubt or nervousness – almost immediately. Sally Atkinson is a lady of diminutive stature who could well have been an Olympic rider. She is an understanding kindly lady, a superb instructor that fixes you with a steely-eyed gaze, refuses to back off and tolerates no nonsense. Sally also has a voice quite capable of being heard over a battlefield. And so in the beginning, or should that really be, in the second beginning and for many months ahead this was the person that with patience, toughness, overwhelming knowledge and resilience was about to shape my future.

Learning to ride under dedicated instruction has just the same underlying principles or processes for any beginner or novice commencing a new sport or activity. It can be as complicated or as straightforward as the person wants, as easy or as difficult as the instructor wishes. Ultimately all that anyone will get out of any activity or sport is what he or she puts into it with the unmistakeable likelihood that this will probably demand a very large percentage of overlap added on. Pushing that extra ten per cent. Digging that little bit deeper.

To develop at any sport it has to be accepted that the idea of following something as a gentle hobby that can be casually picked up and laid down on a whim lacks fundamental drive and passion. As much as those attributes are crucially important it still takes an awful lot more. Many sports psychologists will argue quite correctly that there is no such thing as a natural aptitude, or that anyone has a God given talent at birth. Far too much positive, practical psychological research has been carried out to prove the point. Apparently, until scientists can identify a "talent" gene, it stays that way. Nonetheless, what has been derived from substantial investigations throughout a large number of diverse sports has demonstrated and concluded that it is practice and lots of it that produces performers. A hundred years ago there were specific opinions that would counter this. But thankfully that belongs to a mindset of a hundred years ago. There is now abundant evidence that shows quite clearly that people can keep getting better long after they should have reached their "rigidly determinate" natural limits. Unsurprisingly, the key to this is referred to as "deliberate" practice - sustained periods of deliberate effort to improve performance in a specific domain. No doubt this would immediately conjure up that age old catch all, "ah yes – practice makes perfect". But that would be entirely contrary to the concept of deliberate practice. Because, surprisingly though, deliberate practice is not what most people actually do when they are practicing. The concept of deliberate practice isn't work and it isn't play but something entirely unto itself. It is an activity designed to create and improve performance almost always with the aid of a teacher or instructor. It is highly demanding mentally and heavily physical and it isn't much fun.

Deliberate practice is characterised by a number of different but interlocked elements. High repetition is the important difference between deliberate practice of a task and performing the task for real, when it counts. Two points distinguish deliberate practice from what most people actually do. One is the choice of properly demanding activity in the learning zone. The other is the amount of repetition and that does not mean repeating an activity over and over again. The key is to identify a learning zone, which in reality is not simple then forcing oneself to stay in it as it changes which is even harder. The obvious follow up to this is a high level of feedback because an individual can work on all the technique that they want but if they can't see the results, a couple of things may happen - they won't get any better and they will stop caring! This is when the coach, mentor, instructor provides that crucial opinion. Deliberate practice is above all an effort of focus and concentration, of motivation and that places enormous strains on anyone's mental abilities.

That is what makes it "deliberate" as opposed to mindless repetitive routine. It probably follows inescapably that deliberate practice is a recipe for not having much fun. Being able to do things or endlessly repeating things we know how to do well is enjoyable and that is exactly the opposite of what deliberate practice demands. So instead of doing what we are good at, we should insistently seek out what we're not good at. From there we identify the painful, difficult activities that will make us better. After each repetition the necessary feedback comes whereby whatever isn't right can be repeated. And that process is repeated until mental exhaustion dictates a period of rest. But more importantly the entire concept of deliberate practice is that it is designed specifically to improve an individual's performance and the key word in this characteristic is *designed.*

Instructing, or coaching, in any sport is a profession that requires both art and science. The building blocks for an optimal performance are many and must be constructed in a proper manner, correct sequence to recognise that each individual is different. Some of these building blocks are correct technique, positive mental attitude, and physical fitness, even the consequences of proper diet. However, the cornerstone for this building is precise physiological and psychological training. That is the main reason why any athlete or sports person spends so much time in practice or wherever conditioning is best conducted. For me the building blocks were not only about reconstructing an injured and weakened body, re-educating a damaged brain but being taught as a complete novice a whole new set of skills that required mental agility, co-ordination, balance, stamina and the capability of eventually being able to think very much "outside the box." With the building blocks in place, the design created, the motivation primed I was about to be conditioned or maybe from a more abstract perspective - programmed. What was about to happen over the coming months was tough, demanding, intense, and at times pushed me to physiological and psychological breaking point. In a sense it was a cross between Therapeutic

Riding and Hippotherapy – but at it's most extreme. Typically the association with that term "extreme" also meant
other things – it was going to take perseverance, determination and a shed load of practice. It was also going to be
painful.

§

Derived from the word "hippos", the Greek word for
horse, the term "Hippotherapy" literally means treatment
or therapy aided by a horse. The concept, which has a large
dedicated, following in the United States, apparently finds
its earliest recorded mention in the ancient Greek writings
of Hippocrates. This is a form of physical, occupational and
indeed speech therapy, which uses the characteristic movements of a horse to provide carefully, graded sensory input.
A foundation is established to improve neurological
function and sensory processing, which can be generalized
to a wide range of daily activities. In Hippotherapy, or
Aloka as it is sometimes called, the movement of the horse
is a means to a treatment goal.

The horse's pelvis has the same three-dimensional movement as the human's pelvis at the walk. This three-dimensional movement provides physical and sensory input,
which is variable, rhythmic and repetitive. The variability
of the horse's gait enables the therapist to grade the degree
of input to the patient and use this movement in combination with other treatment strategies to achieve desired
therapy goals or functional outcomes. In addition, the
three-dimensional movement of the horse's pelvis leads to
a movement response in the patient's pelvis, which is
similar to the movement patterns of a human walking. This
in turn improves neurological function and sensory processing, which can be generalized to a wide range of daily
activities and address functional outcomes and therapy

goals. Adults and children with disabilities can improve their posture, muscle tone, coordination, balance, sensory/motor development as well as speech and language skills with Hippotherapy.

Therapeutic riding differs from this in the simple basis that specific riding skills are taught and developed. In an Equine Assisted Activities program, the riding instructor teaches a person with a disability how to ride a horse. However, the environment of the horse can provide more than just riding skills. The programs which offer the equine environment to people with disabilities can teach companionship, responsibility, leadership, vocational, educational skills as well as offer competition venues in the different horse disciplines. Riding a horse provides a unique and often profound recreational or leisure activity for many people. There are many sports which people who have disabilities can participate in for enhancing their lives, which offer social, and physical fitness as addressed in the Special Olympic programs for people with a cognitive disability. There are hundreds of programs around the world as well as many organizations dedicated to the various forms of horse riding or horse care which address many other disabilities that may not have a cognitive element.

The student who interacts with their horse may extend this to others and to form meaningful relationships with people. Building a relationship with an animal is very rewarding in many aspects; for a person with an emotional, social or psychological disability, the trust and loyalty of an animal demonstrates to the student how important they are and then they may extend these attributes to personal relationships. Horses also help people feel in control of their situation because there is a direct correlation between action and reaction. To learn how to care for and ride a horse, a student must also be able to communicate efficiently with the horse and the instructor. In this way, riding is a very social activity, but is less daunting to people who are uncomfortable in social situations. However, the experience of riding a horse is very different. Riding helps to empower people and enables them to connect on a personal level. The sometimes-unpredictable nature of animals and/or assimilated situations also creates a real-life environment in which students will be able to confront fears and make adjustments to situations beyond their control. Without any further question or doubt, what initially began for me as an underlying curiosity to solve a puzzle progressed into a passage to regaining physical fitness and mental agility through the association with marvellous creatures. It was also about to set the stage for an entirely new direction in life.

§

When I stepped up off the mounting block for the first time that morning and my left foot first connected with a stirrup, any apprehension that I may have had about horses in general or riding disappeared, never to return. And so in the beginning, I learned to walk. It hurt. Even while sitting quite still, it became manifestly obvious that the movements carried out required great co-ordination. Then I learned to trot and it hurt more. Eventually the inevitable introduction to a further shift in tempo, the technique changed to a rising trot and that hurt even more – at least for a while. But I persevered. Badly unfit after weeks of inactivity, I could barely manage a couple of laps of the school without being totally out of breath. At the end of some days, I was left physically and mentally drained. For days my muscles ached, unused to the functionality of riding. But this time I managed to sit down without the necessity or recourse to a cushion because I was learning to ride – properly and within a purpose built learning zone with a specific goal in mind.

Individuals have their own way of adapting to appropriate physiological training. This is based on aerobic and anaerobic conditioning, volume and intensity. Accordingly my training or probably more correctly conditioning, as the Americans would call it became a planned process that varied from day to day. It was a bit like the three D approach to conditioning for endurance horses – difficulty, duration and distance, the rule of thumb being to only ever increase one of these at a time and even then only by ten per cent at a time. Inevitably each daily session would start with some gentle walking around the school to warm up the horse. This would be followed by the:

"I'm so looking forward to this – the fun bit!

Really! No – honestly – I am!"

With the horse standing stock still in front of the large dressage mirror, the next ten minutes were spent carrying out exercises to Sally's command. Right hand touch left stirrup, left hand touch right stirrup. And repeat. Stomach crunch forward until my nose touched the horse's head. Now lean back until the back of my head touched the horse's rump. And repeat! Head and neck rotating, shoulder curls. And repeat! Feet out of the stirrups stretch legs down and back, relax. And repeat! But what a difference those warm up exercises made. Because the whole concept of successful riding is based on the correct levels of balance and stability, the warm up exercises also meant a more relaxed approach, sitting deeper in the saddle, tension free, focussed but ready to enjoy every single minute. The added purpose of warm ups is to ensure that the rider is also physiologically prepared and in consequence the likelihood of serious or protracted injury resulting from a simple or minor strain are lessened. Gradually the strength came back, muscles that I never knew existed became honed, stamina increased. As the days passed into weeks, then the weeks into months, the beginner gradually slipped into the past, a rider slowly but confidently began to emerge.

Then one day just as I thought satisfactory progress was being made - my stirrups were taken from me. The entire process started all over again. And that hurt. Exercises intensified. I learned to ride blindfold with no stirrups and hands extended straight out to the sides. The working trot moved to a canter, a canter to walk, walk to canter. More difficult tasks were practiced, developed, including manoeuvres described with such patently obvious terminology like "turn on the forehand and quarters, leg yield, half pass" etc. But in reality, despite the perceived monotony of dressage, a complex riding discipline within its own right, all of those drills were extremely useful techniques, However, despite Sally's expert tuition, it was pretty evident that my potential as a dressage rider, despite the appeal of a top hat and some pretty cool looking attire, was, how should we say, limited!

Then on one beautiful warm afternoon, the big sliding doors of the indoor school were opened up. For a fleeting moment I thought I was about to be set free to ride into the countryside to canter through the fields, the wind in my face, sunlight in my eyes, the hypnotic thumpety - thump of hooves hitting the ground. Wow! Was I wrong? The only place I was set free into was the jump arena. Really! The bubble burst. That was the one place that I definitely did not want to be – freedom or not! Initially I did not relish the idea of jumping over poles and things, especially if I had to be on the horse at the same time as it happened. Even a number of sessions later I still did not take pleasure in the idea but as always student and teacher persevered. I even coped with a jump of about half a metre, managing to stay on the horse – just!

Eventually we did venture out into the countryside where I learned how and where to jump drystane dykes, negotiate streams, deal with traffic and roadwork, open and close gates, assess speed and distance, gauge the nature and type of terrain. It was exhilarating, a bit like a mobile classroom, a virtual teaching session. For the next few months, most of my riding took place outdoors, along tracks, steep forest trails and fields, the duration increasing on each occasion, the difficulty demanding just that little bit more concentration and effort. The weather held nothing back as we jumped logs in the woods or plodded across sticky ploughed fields in snowstorms. Some days it was a canter along the long sweeping stretches of sandy beaches, climbed up dunes, and crossed fields, rivers and roads. In bad weather, it might be under the shelter of the hillside, riding along the field margins, along and under the railway lines. There was always the unmistakable buzz of the zing of steel on stone or tarmac, the rhythmic thump of hooves along field margins. Sometimes when the wind howled and the rain was merciless, it meant a return to seek shelter in the soft security and solace of the indoor school.

Then the endless practice started all over again – circles, serpentines, figures of eight, and gentle jumps, stepping over poles. It was working together in partnership, focussed, and motivated. Each day was very different but it was inevitable that a day would arrive or eventually after weeks of deliberate practice a sense of overconfidence or indifference would creep in. The challenge of endless circuits of the indoor school, the figures of eight, and ten metre circles was becoming routine, boring, the challenge wearing off. Instead of following instructions by crossing from A – F or C – D or whatever, I let Phantom wander around aimlessly at a gentle trot. Exasperated with this display of sluggishness by horse and rider, Sally played her ultimate move. Marching into the centre of the school, jaw thrust forward in her own inimitable manner, the lunge whip in her right hand manifestly obvious.

"Who is that for then", I enquired in a smirking, cocky manner.

"I haven't decided yet", came the quiet but forthright reply.

Phantom and I clicked up a gear – immediately.

That is what a sports psychologist would call extrinsic motivation.

The drive to succeed, impetus, enthusiasm, motivation, apparently comes in two forms - extrinsic and intrinsic. Extrinsic motivation is driven by external factors such as tangible rewards or pressures, rather than for the fun of it. It can also be detrimental because this is derived on the basis that extrinsic motivation may mean rewards and those can decrease internal motivation, as people work to gain the reward rather than because they like doing the work or believe it is a good thing to do. Extrinsic motivation can also mean punishment or threats of punitive measures. These are again more likely to be detrimental or negative. For example, when I do something, I have to explain why I do it. If I am being rewarded extrinsically for doing it, then I can explain to myself that I am doing it for the reward or to get round the threat of punishment. But in effect extrinsic motivations can then change a pleasurable experience into un-enjoyable work. Yet by far, the most effective positive aspect of extrinsic motivation is recognition, and more importantly recognition of competence or ability – that generally comes from one of the fundamental elements of deliberate practice – feedback. In reality though without competence or ability there can never be any further positive extrinsic motivators. However, the concept of extrinsic motivation is diametrically opposed to the internal drivers of intrinsic motivation – impetus from within. Much of current research has shown that there is very little that can induce someone to endure years of pain and sacrifice in deliberate practice unless it was through their own compulsion to succeed. The building blocks so carefully put together a few months previously had reached a point whereby I had become entirely immersed in the task at hand, time had slowed down and the enjoyment heightened. But now the task was beginning to seem effortless, the challenges too easy, routine and boring.

There is little or no doubt that I could have quite simply walked away at that point confident and comfortable in the knowledge that I had taken on the task and reached a reasonable novice level within a short period of time. The fact that I had survived and no longer considered horses to be large scary creatures that breathed fire and smoke from their nostrils was more than an added bonus. But there was something else there perhaps something too difficult to understand or explain. Maybe it was something that was triggered, in what seemed like a long way back, in the dusty recesses of my mind when I lay on a hospital bed. There were no real explanations for a lot of things and truth be known there was no longer any real interest or concern about delving into the spiritual or paranormal worlds or the existence of the void or beings of light. Each time my developing skills matched a challenge I achieved a high. If it was too easy it became boring, too hard and it became frustrating. I wanted to continue to learn more, to develop, master new tasks, seek greater challenges and match those with higher-level equestrian skills. It is the process that parallels the deliberate practice routine of continually pushing past one's current abilities – the search of achieve-ment and chasing the ultimate goal, finding the maximum high - keeping the drive, holding the passion. Yet strangely although the intrinsic motivation was still there, deeply embedded in my psyche somewhere there was little or no particular feeling that I was in full control of what I was actually doing. In one sense the motivation was still highly extrinsic because I had merely sought recognition for reaching a level of competence and that was forthcoming. The first goal achieved!

Perhaps the physiological and psychological conditioning, the robotic brain washing of deliberate practices necessary to fast track someone into a previously alien sport had been extremely effective but then I had also been an easy and willing receptacle. However, a couple things could now happen – there was the possibility that unless I could meet the necessary new challenges for development I probably wouldn't get any better and secondly I was approaching one of the most dangerous situations within the deliberate practice process - that I could stop caring.

The time to take stock of the situation, to decide on a new direction, if any, was fast approaching, the allocated timescale given over to the intensive rider training programme coming to a close. Fortunately an interesting proposition turned up quite unexpectantly soon after and momentarily helped to take my mind away from a decision about my equestrian future. A DVD and book had been commissioned on the subjects of the Dee and Don rivers and valleys. The focal point of attention on the Don would be of a historical nature, emphasis on its dominance as an agricultural producing area whereas the Dee, its origins in the depths of the high Cairngorms and much more rugged would examine the wider aspects of the sporting estates. What was really needed was assistance in filming a stalking party within one of the Deeside estates. If the Highland ponies, or garrons were still being used for extracting the days carcasses, even better. Within a matter of a few days, I had made the necessary arrangements, volunteering to assist with taking the ponies up onto the hill for Peter Fraser, Head Keeper on the Invercauld Estate's Badach and Callater beats. It was a good decision.

As it turns out, the sun must shine on the righteous because an early November morning, despite a frosty start was in glorious sunshine. It was only twenty-two weeks after coming out of hospital and I felt wonderful. I was glad to be back amongst the hills with people I had known for a long time, back within familiar territory, privileged to be working with trained ponies.

The term pony is used rather than horse for the simple reason that the official cut off point that denotes a pony and horse is 14.2 hands high. Garrons can grow slightly higher but no doubt the "showing classes" would frown upon anything above the 14.2hh mark. These ponies tend to be much more heavily muscled than many other breeds, deep chested, heavy bellied, stocky, wide, and with strong short legs. Typically, as with many other breeds there is some question as to the origin of these hardy animals. Arguably, there are three types; those from the island of Barra and the many smaller Hebridean islands, Mainland ponies from Mull and the Scottish Riding or garron. The latter term rather than Highland derives from the Gaelic and is widely used throughout the estates and stalking circles to denote the working breed. But wherever the origin, these ponies can plod along all day.

Originally used for all manner of crofting work, these are colourful equines, sweet natured in disposition, sure footed, very strong and hardy and are perfectly capable of carrying an eighteen stone stag down off difficult terrain. For that reason, there are not many trekking centres in Scotland that do not have a string of Highlands for tourists or beginners to use. There are still carvings by Picts in existence, depicting short, stocky types of pony, with flowing manes, forelocks and tails. Even now the Highland breed has developed very little, the distinctive eel-stripe that runs down the spine an ancient characteristic. There is no better sight in watching these sure-footed animals picking their way down some of the most horrendous terrain possible. But ponies are hard work. It takes the best part of three years following in their mother's or another mare's footsteps before they could be considered suitable for going solo. Although from a traditional viewpoint the pony may be the preferred mode of transport for extraction, the cost and effort in training and indeed maintenance far outweighs the economical viability. Sadly, many estates are now replacing the hardy garrons with more efficient yet less eco-friendly mechanised forms of transport.

As we traipsed through the heather, the sun burst over the summit of Tolmount flooding the glen in bright crystal-clear sunlight. Unaccustomed to being back in the steep hillside surroundings my lungs struggled with the effort but very quickly I found my breath. Legs still gaining strength after the weeks of paralysis and general weakness but now attuned to riding technique ached as we ploughed through the heather. I could easily understand now why hardened cowboys became so terrified of walking any distance on their own legs. Hooves splashed through the mud, boots were soaked, clothing splattered. As for Lady, my movie star garron and companion for the day? Well! She just plodded along in her own inimitable garron laid back shuffle, tacked with the stalking saddle, the Glenstrath-farroch, an unusual piece of handcrafted leatherwork for someone accustomed to the relative simplicity of an English saddle.

As we closed on the foot of Creag an Fhir-Shaigdhe, the radio crackled into life. Our instructions were to stop there, keep the ponies out of sight as Peter crawled into his final shooting position. We ducked down behind a heather clad knoll to wait. Archie and I lay back in the deep heather, savouring mugs of tea. Unfettered, the ponies moved gently around our feet and legs, searching for some tasty morsel. The day lingered. Time stood still. Bar the occasional grunt from one of the ponies, or the gentle tinkling sound from a nearby burn there was no sound. But the music was everywhere. The sun shone down on us. The hills stood out in sharp contrast to the clear blue skies. Had I died at that moment, I would have gone in perfect serene peace.

As Archie and I sat with our backs propped against heather clad banks, we focussed our binoculars on Peter, a few hundred metres away. We could just pick him out, his tweeds or "estate tartan", almost blending in perfectly with the surrounding heather and rocky hillside, his two Springers sitting attentively behind him. A hundred metres below him the small herd of red deer hinds grazed nonchalantly, perfectly oblivious to any human predator above them. I swung my binoculars from Peter to the herd. A spurt of dust was thrown up from the body of one of the hinds, in an instance the bumph of the high velocity round shattered the silence. The hind dropped where it had stood, Instinctively I knew that Peter would be working the bolt on the rifle, a second round clicking into the chamber. Seconds later another bumph shattered the silence. Another hind fell. The herd scattered. The radio crackled into life again.

"Take the horses up now", called Peter in his broad but quiet Aberdeenshire voice.

Within seconds we were on our way. This time there was no path to follow. Instead we worked our way up and across the exposed hillside, negotiating rocks, burns and heather banks. The contours were fierce, the climbing steady and sheer. Had we slipped, there was nothing below us except a tumbling drop all the way down to the end of the loch. But the confident slow moving ponies worked their own way up and over the steep hillside. If they chose to go their way, we let them. On a previous occasion, Lady had taken a tumble down a hillside whilst carrying a heavy stag. After rolling three times down the slope, apparently she simply stood up, grunted, shook herself off, and then carried on. Tough as old boots she was totally unconcerned and unimpressed with her spectacular yet unplanned rapid descent. These are no dressage stars but hard working animals doing what they know best in the terrain that bred them.

If the ascent appeared steep, from my immediate vantage point, the descent looked downright precarious. In fact I looked down in awe at the vertigo-inducing gradient. It's one thing descending steep rocky terrain with no-one to worry about except myself but negotiating ponies laden with deer carcasses over that same ground is another matter. It was wrong to be unduly worried. I should have known. Just as confidently as they had ascended the hillside, the two ponies negotiated the downward slope with ease, picking their own route slowly cautiously through the maze of rock and heather hillocks. We bobbed and weaved past rocky outcrops, over burns, through mud and slippery peat to finally pick up the track that led back towards the lodge. As we reached the well-defined path, we picked up speed, or at least a slightly faster pace – a shuffle to an amble. Then for the next hour we meandered along the track, splashing through burns and mud, Archie in the lead with Josie, me plodding along behind him with Lady. All too soon we were back at the lodge – the day's work over. It had certainly been a privilege to work with Peter, Archie and the ponies. I was saddened to leave but other work called. The impetus to continue riding was heightened, the motivation to maintain the association with horses liberally boosted. Two days later I was back in the riding school, but longing for the wide-open spaces.

For the rest of the year my riding continued, hopefully skills increasing as each day passed. Time alternated between developing my balance, carrying out more complex manoeuvres, increasing my jumping prowess. As the weather deteriorated into December, more time was spent in the indoor school where I concentrated hard but the call of the outdoors stayed with me. In the dark afternoons the school seemed claustrophobic, confining. I longed to be back on the open trails but winter was soon in progress – the hills would have to wait. So I concentrated more, listened harder, learned more as each day passed. Muscles long since attuned to the demands of riding grew stronger. Physical strength and fitness had reached levels that I had not known for a long time. I was as mentally alert as could be expected, totally confident. There was no fear, no trepidation. Sally was happy, pleased with my rapid development. Very soon I was training with instructors under training. As valuable as it was, the indoor school seemed to be becoming a claustrophobic restriction, an understandable necessity, but nevertheless a constriction. Then one day, as we swung into a tight turn Phantom's hind hoof clipped a trotting pole. The horse twisted. In an instant, my balance rocked. As I fought to regain my position, my right ankle bent up and inwards at the same time, damaging ligaments and tendons in the process. Typically, it had to be that joint, so desperately weakened as a result and aftermath of stroke. So it was back to the doctor, then the suggestion of lengthy physiotherapy.

The injury was bad enough for me to have to ease off for a while. Given that the ankles are effective shock absorbers for riding, I had no intention of ending up with permanent damage or even worse risking an operation to fix the tendon or ligament. As the New Year came and went, I took stock of the situation, making plans for he future. I needed to get back riding as soon as possible; the addiction was by now firmly entrenched in me, the decision and desire to continue to develop had become embedded. I was tempted to start the course of physiotherapy but given the experience with a previous physiotherapist decided against the suggestion. In fact the only physiotherapist that I did ever enjoy working with was a long blond haired European television star. However in this case his name was Jake and he was an Austrian Halflinger, a star of the TV series Monarch of the Glen. But that is a different story! As an alternative, I embarked on a rigorous physical training routine for myself. There was no intention of losing the fitness that had taken so long to regain.

Unfortunately it is an unpleasant fact that too many people engaging in various sports don't take the time or effort to improve their own physical fitness. That is not just applicable to horse riding but a whole range of sports. There are of course volumes of information in respect of getting horses fit and in consequence many people simply ignore their own physical condition, which is a great shame. Even with the fastest, lightest titanium constructed racing bike in the world, Lance Armstrong could never have achieved the record number of Tour de France victories unless he was super fit. No doubt many people believe that in riding, all that is necessary is to hang on. That is probably as stupid and un-athletic a statement as a world class darts player saying he needs eight pints of beer and two chicken vindaloos before he is capable of reaching the levels of concentration required for a major competition.

When the injury struck there was a high risk that permanent damage may well have occurred and the only option at that juncture would have been an operation. However, the real advice that was forthcoming, surprisingly originated from a football coach. The unexpected guidance was that I didn't need an operation; what I needed was a proper exercise programme. For the past four months I had been using the same muscles for riding but what my body really needed now was to be more balanced. That made sense especially when I looked back to the day's filming at Invercauld where I had struggled for a while as we plodded through the deep heather and rough terrain. Of course I was fully aware that horses need to be fit to compete at higher levels and fitness for purpose makes then stronger, sounder, more supple, more balanced and in general more athletic overall. Why shouldn't that apply to the riders as well? Performance, athleticism and well-being should be matched!

I imagine that it is the goal of every sportsperson to achieve a satisfactory level of performance, for riders to accomplish that oneness with their horse. Of course that might mean something completely diverse for different riders but in general it is the feeling of co-ordination, balance and communication that comes when rider and horse are on the same wavelength and heading in the same direction. An unfit rider – unfit physically, mentally or emotionally cannot realize oneness. It is possible to strive for it but unless all the pieces of the puzzle, the building blocks are there it will be unachievable. Muscles, co-ordination, ligaments, balance and brain all need to be functioning as well as possible.

Riders expect, demand their horses to be healthy, supple and generally fit to prevent injury and to maximise performance. If one member of that partnership, combination is tired then the absolute requirement for communication will undoubtedly break down. So with that simple premise in mind I set about indulging in some serious physical training for a relatively short period of six weeks because in real terms, that duration of intensity, concentrated activity is all that is required for a reasonably healthy human being to regain a degree of enhanced physical and mental fitness. But the crucial components are that it takes resolution, determination. More importantly it also needs to be structured, designed. And that takes us all the way back to the entire concept of deliberate practice!

For weeks it was a case of working hard to recover from the injury. Then as the winter passed I was given and took the opportunity to ride a selection of quite different horses, the style of riding most often defined a lot simply by each horse's own characteristics, personalities and of course breed. These were great experiences, invaluable. Similarly, as I wandered from place to place, inevitably I would come across a wide range of people from across the equestrian divide, many of whom displayed many of the characteristics and temperaments of the horses they owned or rode. Truth be known, some of those attributes were downright odd!

On one particular occasion, as we negotiated the edges of ploughed fields, a young ride leader, attempting to engage me in idle chat asked quite bluntly,

"Do you jump?" she sniffed.

"Me? Nah! Only if someone sneaks up behind me and says – Booo!" responding in a lighthearted manner.

My attempt at humour was completely lost as she continued haughtily,

"You should try endurance then, that's for people who can't jump."

I had no idea what she was speaking about.

"Really?" I enquired, "Whats that then?"

"Well its sort of charging about the countryside for ages with maps. Bunch of weirdos apparently who are just as fizzy or as hyperactive as the Arab horses they ride. Definitely not dressage or eventing material I would say," she sniffed back.

"Really? Sounds like a lot of fun to me."

As she turned to look at me in a bemused almost condescending manner, I said nothing but smiled as broadly as I could. It confuses people!

It was just about then that her horse took an immediate dislike to the coloured plastic bucket at the entrance to the stubble field. After a nifty bit of hoof work and a quite rapid, impressive albeit uncontrolled turn on the forehand, her horse put its head down. And bolted for all its life. Of course, the young horse I was on, sensed the mood, no doubt sniffed the hint of fear from its riding mate, then tried to pull the same stunt. Luckily I caught the signals just as the rapid 180 degrees pirouette inspired turn started, then managed to put the brakes on fast. But as the horse started to spin I felt a short sharp stabbing pain go through my right ankle. The damage had been done - again. Oh well! Obviously had a design flaw somewhere!

The Run for the Roses

"Many are stubborn in pursuit of the path they have chosen, few in pursuit of the goal."

SEVEN months previously I had been carted out of hospital in a wheelchair as a changed person. Now four months after starting the intensive riding programme, I walked out of the riding centre a much better person. I was mentally and physically fit, my metabolism functioning on levels close to Olympic standard. Magnetic Resonance Imagery (MRI) scans showed muscle and bone density at levels twenty years below my age. Blood and chemical tests displayed results that showed the good bits higher than average; the bad stuff lower than average. During a routine check up at the hospital, the results confirmed there was nothing much wrong with me. Surprisingly, the results also showed that there was little or no explanation for the stroke.

In general terms, with the exception of the ankle injury I really was in pretty good shape. However, according to a local GP, there was a suggestion that if I did continue riding at any level there was a high risk of permanent damage to the joint. But the levels of exercise and the benefits to health and enjoyment far overshadowed the hazard. Correspondingly, a sports orthopaedic surgeon provided better encouragement but also indicated quite categorically that I would probably never be much more than two steps away from the pain relieving cortisone injection into the tendon or that each ride might just trigger the inevitable operation. Whichever way, the benefits far outweighed the risk. Whatever! I needed more riding. Crucially I needed another challenge. Looking back to the comments expressed by that young ride leader, and the fact that dressage, show jumping or eventing held little or any interest for me, the concept of endurance riding entered the thought process. It was time to do some serious research.

Endurance riding, the sport of a million steps as it is known out in the Arabian Gulf is forged from the basics of good old-fashioned horsemanship and high tech innovation. It is the sport of the pioneer, the seeker of adventure and challenge. As a sport it arose from the desire of people to take their partnership with the horse to new limits of achievement. At its purest level, or at the peak of competitive distances it is the challenge of riders and horses against the natural elements, the management of horse and rider's skills over difficult terrain. As an equestrian discipline it has rolled back the frontiers of veterinary science. It is probably difficult to argue as to the exact origins or what might constitute equestrian endurance since over centuries man has achieved great distances on horseback. Apparently one rider in the 19th Century covered the distance from Fealar Lodge in Perthshire to Stonehaven in Aberdeenshire and back again in less than twenty-four hours. Even as the crow flies that is in excess of 150 miles. Of course there is always Dick Turpin's flight from London to York? In the history of exploration in the United States of America Cavalry units were routinely required to undertake 200-mile patrols where the basic requirements were for man and horse to suffer long periods of isolation and self-sufficiency during prolonged journeys across the vast untamed wildernesses.

In Virginia, on the east coast of America the Old Dominion endurance ride was born of an idea based on a dream to have it follow the structure of those self same cavalry rides. At one of the original organiser's request a Cavalry Award was devised for the horse and rider team that rode the ride with the least outside assistance. In later years the criteria changed to the horse and rider combination that was judged as in the best condition among the competitors that rode "independently". In 1976, 56 horses began the race. Despite temperatures rising from 60 degrees to a sweltering 86 degrees and a dripping humidity of 64%, 41 completed the ride.

The Western States Trail Ride, popularly called the Tevis Cup Ride, is the oldest modern day endurance ride, having been held annually since 1955. As such, it has been the inspiration and model for the most challenging endurance rides worldwide. Wendell Robie, an Auburn businessman and devoted rider of the Sierra high country, organised the first ride. Many people in the 1950s doubted that any modern-day horse could cover the rugged trail from Lake Tahoe, Nevada to Auburn, California in a single day. Wendell and a few of his friends proved them wrong in August of 1955. He continued to hold the ride annually thereafter and organised the Western States Trail Foundation to preserve the 100-mile trail and the Ride. The Tevis Cup trophy is awarded to the person who completes the 100-Mile One-Day course in the shortest amount of time and whose horse is in sound condition and "fit to continue." The Tevis Cup was named for Lloyd Tevis (1824 - 1899) by his grandson Will Tevis, a prominent San Francisco businessman and early benefactor of the Ride, and was first awarded in 1959 to Nick Mansfield, riding Buffalo Bill, an eleven-year-old TB Cross gelding. As within many other nation's long distance events, Arabian horses now dominate the leading results.

The American Endurance Ride Conference (AERC) was founded in 1972 as the national governing body for long distance riding in the United States. Over the years it has developed a set of rules and guidelines designed to provide a standardised format with strict veterinary controls. At the same time it has sought to avoid the rigidity and complexity so characteristic of many other equine disciplines. From its beginnings in the American West, the AERC has spread roots both nationally and internationally. The AERC sanctions more than 700 rides each year throughout North America. In 1978 the Federation Equestre Internationale (FEI) recognized endurance riding as an international sport, and since that date the U.S. and Canada have regularly swept the team and individual medals. In 1993 Endurance became the fifth discipline under the United States Equestrian Team (USET).

On the UK mainland, endurance riding falls under the auspices of two specific organisations, the Scottish Endurance Riding Club (SERC), and south of the border Endurance Great Britain (EGB) rules the roost with a rod of iron. In 1982 Candy Cameron formed the Highland Long Distance Riding Club, which eventually became SERC and now comprises of 9 semi-autonomous branches throughout Scotland. EGB was formed in 2001 through the amalgamation of the British Endurance Riding Association (BERA) and the Endurance Horse and Pony Society of Great Britain (EHPS). Despite its comparative newness, the sport in the UK has risen in popularity with levels of competitive distances increasing ever since. The Arab Horse Society also runs the Arab Marathon in Wiltshire as an annual event. Theoretically, both national organisations should share a common goal, interlinked set of rules and principles. Sadly, ever so occasionally, the amateur, childish politicising of some self appointed officialdom creates unnecessary time wasting cross border friction where ultimately it is the rider that suffers. But I suppose it's a sad fact that some people need to thrive on officialdom!

As most endurance people will only be too quick to willingly point out - the one thing that endurance riding isn't – is that it is not an amble in the countryside. Even at the lower levels of what for some obscure reason is known as a pleasure ride in Scotland or a non competitive ride (NCR) in EGB parlance riders are required to undertake basic vetting for the horses and meet minimum and maximum speed categories. Endurance riding can be loosely defined as "competitive long-distance riding" and endurance rides have been in existence in Britain since the early 1970's. The sport has evolved quickly over the years to a point where success at top level requires an almost scientific attention to detail in terms of feeding and training; however it still provides plenty of scope for the majority of riders whose ambition is to simply enjoy the sport to the best of their own and horse's ability. Despite the lonely hours of repetition and gruelling distances, the sport within the UK and on an international level continues to grow. In the words of Suzy Kelley, "It can be all the nasty things in the world, but it's still fun. Why else would we keep coming back unless we're masochists?" And that could well be true. But in a more forthright hypothesis, "Sometimes its real disappointing, but it's like any sport - there's only one winner, and the rest would like to be." And as for the participants? Well, I guess there just might be a touch of the odd, weird and downright hyperactive.

"But psychologically it's the same type of people who do marathons," said Roxanne Greene, herself a veteran of more than 500 endurance races. "Not all horses can do it and not all people can do it."

Henceforth, armed with a reasonable bit of research and background knowledge, the next logical step was to attempt participation, reluctantly join the movement. However one major hurdle existed – no horse! Most certainly as a complete stranger, no one was going to lend me one either. So it was the case of doing the next obvious, volunteer as a helper, gather information, watch and listen and as Bomford said, " . . . .*time spent in reconnaissance is always time worth spent!*" The experience of assisting at a few rides, acting mainly as a control point or road crossing steward was good experience. It was inevitable that the obligatory levels of a clique would become readily apparent but I imagine that officialdom anywhere has a level of stature to maintain! Of course it was also inevitable that being a man in an equestrian world that is populated largely by women might create some opportunities for the self-indulgent hypocrites or "tittering" classes to ponder over. Nevertheless, these were useful exercises from which a lot of vital information was gathered, and from the latter a lot of amusement derived.

It was about this time in early April that I started to seriously consider getting my own horse. Initially, I looked at the possibility of getting one on loan but this practice to me can be somewhat restrictive and in too many occasions the obligation all ends up in tears. Instead, I hunted through various web sites, magazines until I found a few suitable horses. Normally by the time I had narrowed these down, the sale was gone. For a while, I considered giving up the quest but I really had to find something that was suitable for my future purposes as I was keen to slowly commence developing some serious endurance work. Of course as usual fate stepped in. By mid April a 16.2hh grey Connemara cross Thoroughbred named Jarrow walked into my life. He officially became known as Spirit of Jarrow in recognition of the workers crusade or their protest march to freedom from Jarrow on Tyneside to London. The name seemed appropriate somehow.

As anyone knows, Ireland is synonymous with horses. It is an ideal country for breeding horses, owing to its mild moist climate, lush grazing and the limestone in the soil. From Ireland come acclaimed racehorse trainers, champion jockeys and some very formidable racehorses. It is also home to the Connemara. But Southern Ireland remains as it always has been, a land of awesome starkness and beauty, of mountains which show no green, of bogs which bear but sedges, of coasts which have no shelter from the Atlantic and of small enclosures which have but stone walls and fuchsia hedges. This is where the Connemara pony continues to live and breed. In spite of many and various infiltrations of outside blood over the years such as Arabians and Thoroughbreds to produce size, speed, strength and stamina it still retains those self same qualities, which have enabled it to survive the hardships of its natural habitat. This native breed, closely similar to our own Highland, or garron, the Connemara pony, *ponaidh,* which in Irish Gaelic simply means small, comes from County Galway. They are a hardy breed, good looking and very tough. Anyway, the Connemaras – and according to Ireland's "Horse Hollerer", these are horses that go through, around or over anything. There was nothing to suggest that a Connemara x TB couldn't make an endurance horse – at least not to any reasonable novice level anyway.

Determined that I was going to take my time with Jarrow, patience became the keyword. His background was mixed with some eventing and jumping. But he was tough, resilient, willing and keen to please and retained a character all of his own. He was also a belligerent horse whose groundwork manners sometimes left a lot to be desired but he was protective and occasionally demonstrated his panache for lashing out at strangers that might just come a little too close to either him or me. Obviously issues existed with roots etched deep from the past. But never at any time did he ever demonstrate any aggression towards me nor did he ever fail me whilst out riding. He could go through, around or over anything! Consequently one very important aspect did emerge - he taught me a whole shed load of knowledge. With that also came some hard-bitten experiences as we meandered through the rest of the year riding out into the steep glens and forests of Angus, explored the hillsides of Dreish and Mayar and climbed into the summits and moors of Lethnot.

On one occasion we were on the perceptible line of a faded, rocky, water logged track that contoured the hillside. On my right the heather clad hillside swept almost vertically upwards to the summit cairn. On my left the slopes plunged steadily down to the valley floor, cut by the ravine and its crashing waters. In front of me were the wide, open heather clad moors that linked the side of Craig Duchray at fourteen hundred feet with the descent into Hunthill. To my left great black clouds were gathering very quickly over Tamhilt. Thunderclaps filled the air, the change in atmospheric pressure evident as the thunderstorm headed our way. The horses were jumpy. Jarrow turned his head towards the gathering storm as I quickly debated the options. There was only one – get the blue blazes out of there as fast as possible – now! We turned in automatic unison. Then for the next four kilometres we descended the steep hill track as the electric storm chased after us. The thunder grew louder. By now great streaks of forked lightning were crashing behind us. Paul dismounted to lead a frenzied Molly down the track. Still riding Jarrow I ploughed on, skidding as we cleared the steepest section, the horse seemingly knowing that we needed to be off that hillside very, very quickly. The Land Rover and trailer crept into sight. Only ten more minutes! As we reached the vehicle, hurriedly tied the horses to the trailer, the thunderstorm, like some great malevolent demon crashed over the summit of Craig Duchray. The downpour that followed was intense. For the next 45 minutes we sheltered in the back of the vehicle with trembling hands holding mugs of tea as the thunder and lightning roared over us. The entire glen disappeared in the deluge of rain, obliterated by the severity of the electric storm. It was mid June, the morning weather chart was wrong but another training ride was over. The horse and rider combination appeared to be holding!

So the days passed. Sometimes the sun was merciless as we sweltered under unusually balmy summer skies, at other times the wind howled and the rain was relentless. The idea of endurance competition did not at any time enter my head nor did I have any real interest in returning to volunteer at any rides. I was perfectly happy doing my own thing, exploring the hills and glens on horseback, savouring each experience. But always we would go just a little further, maybe a little faster, pushing the levels, stretching the boundaries, learning and growing. It wasn't until later in that year when I inadvertently bumped into an enthusiastic hill walker that the idea of pushing those boundaries just a little bit further sprang to mind. Regaled by tales of self sufficient walkers undertaking their own form of endurance by traversing Scotland from west to east, an idea slowly began to foster a plan.

Somewhere back in time someone decided to walk from the west coast of Scotland to the east. Why that particular direction was chosen is anyone's guess, why anyone wanted to do it in the first place is equally beyond me. Then again, probably not! But it happened and from then on the west-east transit of Scotland has become an annual land-mark in the dedicated hill walkers' calendar. Presumably, the starting point of the Ardnamurchan Peninsula was selected as it was close to the most westerly point of land on the British mainland. On a similar presumption, Scurdie Ness, near Montrose was chosen as the concluding point for the journey through the hills and countryside because maybe it is the logical culmination of a route that would be infinitely more enjoyable than plodding along the main roads and monotonous landscape of Buchan to terminate at Peterhead, the most easterly. Of course I might be very wrong!

In the early days, the walk became known as the Ulti-mate Challenge, the name originating from the outdoor clothing company that originally helped to sponsor the event. At a later date, the annual pilgrimage fell under the auspices of The Great Outdoors (TGO) magazine. As far as I am aware there is no prize, no winners, it is simply a challenge somewhere along the alleged ethos of endurance riding – to complete is to win. On a similar vein, there are rules although these appear to be much more unceremoni-ous and probably impossible to police without massive formalisation and associated logistics. No doubt imposed legislation would destroy the enjoyable nature of the challenge, negate the relaxed informal and non-competitive approach that has made the walk immensely popular. Anyway! In the absence of any prizes for speed, I assume that the challenge is undertaken for the satisfaction of completing an endurance walk across some of the most isolated, arduous yet enjoyable, picturesque landscape in the British Isles? For the most part the participants can choose any route they wish, most opting to follow the same old drover's roads and hill passes that criss-cross the nation. Whichever speed they choose to walk at or how many places they decide to overnight is a matter for their own discretion. For walkers setting forth on The Great Outdoors Challenge the distance is not much different to an optimal car journey – a shade over two hundred miles.

Now driving a car from one side of the country to the opposite is comparatively straightforward. Even depending on how quick or scenic a journey the traveller wishes to indulge in, there is a minimal choice of routes. For the walker, the options increase quite dramatically but are again dependent on the difference between easy plodding along the edges of busy country roads or negotiating arduous time worn tracks through open moorland and over craggy hillsides. Most opt for the latter, and where possible or feasible, the intention being to keep away from the hustle and bustle of traffic.

Scurdie Ness Lighthouse is not the most easterly point of the Scottish mainland, nor is Ardnamurchan Point the most westerly. On the east coast, the dubious honour of being the most easterly point on the mainland goes to a rocky outcrop on the Keith Inch, which lies almost due east, from the centre of Peterhead, *The Blue Toon.* On the other side of the mainland, the geographical privilege of being the furthest westerly point goes to another rocky outcrop named Corrachadh Mor, *the great tapering field.* Solely as a point of interest, this piece of rock is actually 35 kilometres further west than Lands End in Cornwall. Ardnamurchan Point in actual fact is located a couple of hundred metres north and east of there and just happens to be the most accessible point. In fact a straight line drawn exactly along a bearing of 270 degrees or due west from Scurdie Ness Lighthouse would miss Ardnamurchan Point by about eight and a half kilometres, the latter being too far north. In practice, the same line would terminate on the mainland somewhere near Auliston Point on the Morvern Peninsula, just above a tiny island named Eilean Uillne, which again is nowhere near being the furthest west. However, by tradition, the starting point is generally Ardnamurchan Point, the route concluding at Scurdie Ness, near Montrose. I still have no idea why!

Depending on the choice of route through the Cairngorms, the nominal distance is just around the two hundred miles mark and a good couple of week's worth of hiking. If walkers could do it, then why couldn't someone on a suitable horse? That seemed a reasonable contest. The seeds were sown, the gauntlet thrown down. From that innocuous meeting the first ever Trans Scotland 200 mile Endurance Ride was born. The challenge being to ride a horse over the same route as the walkers chose - two hundred odd miles of difficult, arduous isolated terrain but in reverse, that being from east to west. Oh! And just as an afterthought – you are going to have to do it a whole lot faster! It was also going to take an awful lot more planning and preparation than merely lacing up a pair of hiking boots and then toting a "ruck" across Scotland. But that laid the basis of the plan for development. When the master plan finally took control it was with almost military precision - it was also going to be a demanding, tough, myopic, intense and at times absolutely unforgiving extrinsic driver. As for me? Other than the promised bunch of red roses in recognition of the award given to American riders there would be no prizes, no rosettes. In terms of a decision to proceed, to accept the challenge, to make the run for the roses - well, it was as simple, spontaneous and "uncomplicated" as that.

Most people would argue that in theory the shortest distance between two points is a straight line. They would of course be correct in one aspect but entirely wrong in another. Ordnance Survey maps are built on the Transverse Mercator projection – flat earth. Although the principle is simple, straight-line measurement does not allow for the distances covered in negotiating slopes or gradients, nor does it take into account the natural terrain.

$$Dist = \sqrt{(E^1 - E^2) + (N^1 - N^2)}$$

Simple Pythagorus!

Consequently, planning a major route across country had to be a much more complicated and serious matter than just simply looking at a map then arbitrarily drawing a line. If for no other reason, difficult as it may be for some people to understand, walkers are well able to negotiate terrain that a horse might find impossible. In fact the planning took the best part of six months with a huge amount of time taken up in harsh practical exploration. Even with the benefits of satellite photography or imagery, 3 dimensional modelling, there can never be any substitute for spending some time in walking sections of the terrain, following Bomford's principle – time spent in reconnaissance! In consequence far from being a straight line from one side of the country to the other, the final route with a number of alternatives available, and emergency detours identified looked more like a twisting winding snake where some sections proceeded north-eastwards rather than heading due west. As winter fast approached, the obligatory time for horses to relax in some well deserved recuperation, provided the ideal opportunity to finalise the last pieces of cross-country navigation. The route was optimised, the stage and crewing points set out, paddocks arranged, accommodation prepared. The start date established for early May, to coincide with the anniversary of the day that I had gone into hospital – the day that my life had irrevocably altered. The plan was now firmly in process.

Probably one of the most important aspects of any undertaking is the necessity for a good support or back up crew. Within the realms of endurance riding competition whether that be Competitive Rides, (CTR) or gated or Endurance Rides, (ER), a support team or "crew" as they are known in endurance circles can be the difference between success and failure. I had recognised at a very early stage that a competent crew would be absolutely imperative. Even then there were huge differences between a CTR and the Trans Scotland. For at start I would be unaccompanied, there would be no markings along the tracks; navigation would be my own responsibility. The fact that I would be on my own comparatively isolated for long periods in near wilderness terrain with just a horse for company didn't actually bother me in the slightest. What was important was the recognition that if something should happen to either the horse, or me, at least some assistance wouldn't be too far away. Any suggestions of irresponsibility had to be definitively minimised. One slip, one error would probably ensure that I would be heavily criticised, no doubt willingly and hastily pilloried by the equestrian world. More importantly, as we were to be travelling very light, looking for a rapid traverse rather than a slow methodical trek the most fundamental task for the crew would be a simple concept - to be ready and waiting for our arrival at the end of each designated stage or carefully arranged crewing point with everything required to ensure that we carried on – sound at the trot – fit to continue!

The most motivated athletes or sports people may be difficult to live with but they have to be single minded about what they are doing. Nothing gets in the way of the plan. And so it was. Whether I was consciously aware that I was becoming more detached as time wore on is a separate debate. There was one sure thing. Nothing was going to get in my way. Nothing was going to stop the plan. I was committed, totally. By the end of the year, a rigorous but sensibly achievable training plan had been prepared for both Jarrow and myself. All too quickly New Years Day arrived. Within a week of the start of the year the plan went into action. I started the work up knowing that theoretically we still had the worst of the winter weather to contend with. But winter was kind. Early morning freezing mist and hard frosts soon gave way to brighter clearer days. Snowfall was rare or minimal. Usually by mid morning at least, the temperatures had risen sufficiently to allow a decent session out in the country. Every other day we bobbed and weaved our way through forest tracks, along narrow roads and across fields Conditioning at its best, the details logged to a spreadsheet whereby I could keep an accurate account of the exercise, dutifully noting progress.

Horses are different from humans – we all know that! Typically there are volumes of information regarding the means to achieve fitness for horses. No doubt each person has his or her own opinion, individual approaches to a subject that generates a lot of diverse debate. For example the Americans would differentiate between training and conditioning, where the first relates to groundwork, handling, manners, dealing with issues. Conditioning relates to the actual process of physically fittening the horse. Conversely in the UK racehorses are trained to race, show jumpers, trained to jump, the assumption being that training is the fittening process. Perhaps it is all really down to semantics but it is usually this aspect, the fittening process that will prompt the debate. Horses are animals and as such are subject to emotion. They are just as likely to have a bad day as anything else or get sour with over zealous, regimented conditioning. The important item of advice given to me is to know how much a horse can take, when to back off a bit, and to stay within that comfort zone. It is not too difficult to accept that a horse in rest is also a horse getting stronger. Horses also have tremendous memory capabilities and that can be both advantageous and detrimental to the levels and/or mode of training and conditioning that they are subjected to. It therefore goes without saying that these can also affect the rider's progress, safety and capability in just the same manner.

A genuine problem in understanding equine fitness is that it is a subjective term. It is very hard to put a number on something such as fitness and be objective about it. Being able to identify something, or how far we have to go along a line between unfit and one hundred percent or maximum fitness is impossible. According to Dr David Marlin of the University of Bristol, horses probably never reach maximum fitness. This is because horses exercised intensely and for long periods may develop other problems that cause the rider or trainer to ease back. These problems can range from behavioural issues or physical problems including depression, loss of appetite, reduced rather than improved performance or lameness. Dr Marlin also states that in consequence, we probably train horses too hard by working them too frequently and that we could achieve the same levels of fitness but with less exercise.

Just as the human being needs a sporting mind as much as a sporting body, the horse needs to be mentally alert with an assertive mind. Mental attitude and well-being are paramount to good performance. A fit healthy horse enjoys making use of its fitness. The better the horse is feeling the more it will want to test its place or instinctive dominance in competition. That manifests itself in wanting, and the operative word here, is "wanting" to go faster and further than the rest. Of course, that bears just a shade in similarity to the intrinsic motivation of the human individual. If

endurance horses need to be strong, fit, fiercely individual-
ist, determined and independent, then it naturally follows
that to meet those characteristics or attributes, so do the
riders. As the Greek cavalryman, Xenophon said,

*"Having made sure that the horses are in good condition,
the next business is to train the men."*

For me, the "plan" was wheeling along. With the full
knowledge that I would be subjected to some pretty rigorous physical demands during the Trans Scotland I devot-
edly started my annual six-week rider's exercise
programme. Thankfully, I could manipulate my working
hours to suit the rigorous training. By mid February,
confidence in Jarrow's conditioning increased as each day
progressed. Confidence increased sufficiently enough to
register an entry for the Grampian Branch of SERC's first
endurance ride of the year at Kirkhill Forest, near Aberdeen.
Perhaps the confidence levels were too high or expectations
were too great. In any event the ride was a near disaster
that left me suitably humiliated.

Now the routine for an endurance event is quite simple.
Trailers are lined up in sensible spacing to allow horses to
be unloaded then tethered to the side. This allows horses
to be handled individually without risk of bumping into
each other. It also allows riders and handlers sufficient
room to get on with the routine aspects of grooming and
tacking up without bumping into each other. Unfortunately
the distances are never far enough apart to disguise the
occasional sniping remark. But hey! I have heard a lot worse
at some other sporting events. The next stage is to present
the horse for a veterinary inspection. For a Pleasure or
Training Ride such as the Kirkhill venue was, all that needed
to be done was to make sure the horse could stand obedi-

ently and long enough for his heart rate to be taken and logged. The rider then leads the horse at a jog around a set of cones some 30 metres away from the vet or competent person, across their line of sight then back towards them. This allows a clear view of the gait, where any lameness of stiffness that might be prevalent can be identified. Quite correctly any indication of unsoundness would mean immediate elimination. Now because Jarrow tended to err on the side of being somewhat "awkward" at times, I decided that the best approach would be to have him tacked up in bridle and bit, knowing full well that he would be instantly calmed and easier to manoeuvre through the vetting. I relaxed at the thought - almost correct!

The fact that the venue, parking and trot ups were in the car park of the Scottish Agricultural College at Craibstone, near Aberdeen didn't for one-minute cause me any thought for worry. It should have. At the point of placing the bridle over Jarrow's nose, a massive pig unseen in the field above the car park let out a god awful piggy squeal followed by a series of snorts. Jarrow's ears went up like missiles ready to be blasted skywards. Just at the moment as I reached towards him either the pig sent out a defiant blast of internal gases or the wind caught the scent of porcine manure and wafted it right over us. Whatever it was, this was just too much for Jarrow. His neck shot up, his head turned sharply, the equi-ties attaching the lead rope to the trailer snapped and off he went.

"Loose horse! Loose horse!" The cry went up.

I went red.

Half of the SERC helpers went after him. For ten minutes Jarrow trotted back and forth along the fence line completely fascinated by the huge lump of gammon on the other side. Any attempt to catch him up, he firmly resisted. Obviously he had found a new friend and for the odd moment, we all assumed that at any given minute Jarrow was going to leap the fence. What might happen after that didn't bear thinking about? Anyway the combined resources of half the Grampian branch's helpers managed to get the horse under control whereby he was returned to the trailer, firmly chastised and tethered with a double set of ties. Not satisfied with just a head collar, I put the heavy rope halter on top – just to make sure. Jarrow was then frog marched, if you can call it that, to the vetting.

"What's your horse's name?" asked the competent person, not looking at the sheet.

"Erm, it was Jarrow, now he's called Porky," I muttered back.

"Really," replied the competent person, "Why do you call him Porky?"

"Because he .....erm likes pigs" I choked, "Do you want me to do the trot up now?"

Fighting back a burst of hysterical laughter, I almost tripped over the lead rope.

Now strangely, after all the consternation he had caused, Jarrow vetted in with a heart rate of 38, which indicated a more than reasonable level of calmness. Me? I was on the verge of a nervous breakdown. Gasping for breath after chasing him along the fence, suitably humiliated, I thought about going home in disgrace. But not quite ready to give up, I optimistically assumed that things could only get better. In fact I was wrong again - it got a whole lot worse. At the timekeeper, I realised that I had left the vet sheet in the Land Rover so trotted back up to get it. My temporary crew for the day had disappeared with the sheet and could not be found. I then missed my starting slot so took the opportunity to trot Jarrow up and down the hill for a few minutes at the side of the car park as a warm up. It must have impressed someone. For some incomprehensible reason, one of the branch committee members gave me a veiled warning about barging past other riders on the course ahead. At that juncture in time, I wallowed in the prospect that my endurance career was almost over before it had started. Barge past other riders on the course? Holy sheesh kebabs, at this rate I would be lucky if I got over the sodding start line.

Anyway we clattered off at a sedate pace, passed through the tunnel under the dual carriageway without a care in the world, then worked our way along the back roads at a leisurely trot. A partly overgrown farm track clearly adorned with the hoof prints of numerous riders ahead of us led gently towards the tree line. Before reaching the main forest track, we negotiated a narrow muddy track, churned up by the horses in front. I had calmed down by this point, dismissing each low-lying branch that threatened decapitation at any time, as all part of the adventure. I really started to enjoy myself. Once on to the hard wide solid forest track, we kicked up a gear. The multitude of walkers, unleashed dogs and Lycra clad cyclists all added to the fun and I smiled broadly at each passer-by. Confuse people? It certainly does!! Nevertheless, Jarrow being confronted by a wide range of possible distractions was a valuable exercise, the more exposure to distracting influences the better. By the time we reached Control Point 1, my watch reasoned we had easily bought a good six minutes to hand. Confidence soared! Accompanied by two other riders, we were for all intents and purposes actually catching up with the three riders seen just ahead of us. Then slowly we dropped down through the forest until we reached a junction, which the rider "talk around" declared as:

"Ignore track left, take right turn – very steep climb ahead."

We swung right to be confronted with a fairly steep hill. Enthusiastically, Jarrow went yeee-haaah as we hit the climb at an impressive canter. It was too impressive. Overjoyed at the exhilarating climb, we went careering past the next turn off to the left that led up into a narrow path through the trees. It was probably about five hundred metres later when I managed to eventually stop. In all fairness the two strips of red and white tape indicating the turn was almost hidden. The three riders we had seen ahead of us earlier had actually made the same mistake.

A quick review of the map confirmed the turn off had been missed, so I turned Jarrow to face back. He had other ideas. Clearly the horse had anticipated that we had followed the correct route, recognised the outward path then reasoned that this was in fact the homeward bound route. He turned all right but refused point blank to budge an inch further. Try as I might he would not move back towards the narrow turn off. Time was ticking past all to quickly, making me realise that there was now no margin to spare. My patience snapped. I jumped off, jogged along the track with Jarrow in tow, found a suitably large rock near the foot of the narrow track to stand on then jumped unceremoniously into the saddle. I turned Jarrow towards the climb. Without any further bidding we hit the steep muddy ascent at a reasonable speed. As Jarrow climbed over the banks with ease, two walkers moved over to let us past. As I looked down to thank them, the elderly gentleman simply looked back up at me and shook his head. At that precise moment in time, I think I knew exactly what he meant.

The rest of the ride went well until my so-called "guide" who had allegedly reconnoitred the route the day before missed a further narrow turn off. Just shortly after this at Control Point 2 we parted company to go our separate ways. Thankfully, now on our own, for the next five or six kilometres we trotted along narrow paths at our own momentum. My ankle was beginning to cause some discomfort, making riding at any greater speed very uncomfortable. But I persevered. As we reached Control Point 1, I breathed a sigh of relief, safe in the knowledge that we were finally on the final leg of the course. At this point however, my right foot was very badly weakened - in fact the pain sufficiently harsh enough to render little or no feeling as I put pressure into the stirrup. By the time we reached the edge of the forest, approaching the side roads, my foot was entirely numb, dangling uselessly. Balance kept me in the saddle, nothing more, as we trotted the final few kilometres back to the tunnel. If there is one thing that a horse does know, and that's the way home, so I struggled on, let Jarrow set the pace. All too soon we were clattering up the incline from the tunnel. Moments later we crossed the finish line where unusually I smiled collecting my vetting time paperwork from the timekeeper. Within thirty minutes we had put Jarrow, by now a seemingly very well behaved horse through the vetting procedure where he logged a final heart rate of forty. He had given his best, showed no signs of any discomfort or lack of fitness. Proudly, at least if not somewhat humbled, I collected my first rosette from the administration caravan. Mistakes had been made but one thing was for certain, I had learned a great deal and if it could be helped in any way those mistakes would never be repeated. An hour later we left the venue having made some new acquaintances, gleaned masses of useful information then departed to the calls of:

"See you at Durris in two weeks time."

I was pleased.

Two days later Jarrow stiffened up on his hind legs.

I was devastated.

Alarm bells started to ring immediately. As it turned out, six months of training, conditioning, planning and complete focus on a goal was about to go out the door in one heart wrenching, mind numbing swoop. The run for the roses was about to become perilously close to being a non-starter.

The Final Countdown

"Face to face, out in the heat. Hanging tough staying hungry".

Jarrow was rested for a couple of days as we assessed the situation. The general consensus being that possibly the ride coupled with the trailer journey home might have caused the stiffness. Jarrow was a poor traveller with a tendency to kick out quite a lot; perhaps he had knocked a joint during transit. But the swelling or fluid build up on two hind joints left a lot of room for apprehension. So, he was rested for a few more days, equipped with magnetic boots at night then generally pampered for the period. Within a couple of days the swelling had gone. Perhaps the initial assessment had been correct – the injury temporary. Slightly relieved we started the preparation for the forthcoming Durris ride the following week. By this time I was really looking forward to the event, keen to extend the distance if possible, sufficiently so that I drove up to the venue then carried out a short reconnaissance of the first part of the route. Apart from having to negotiate a couple of farm gates, there was nothing that unduly concerned me. In fact I firmly believed that the terrain would suit Jarrow perfectly. With lessons learnt from Kirkhill, confidence levels increased once more. For the rest of that week we hacked out on the same basis every other day, concentrating on climbing and forest work. It is an excellent way to build impulsion, to teach a horse to use his back end, developing strength and wind without stressing his legs. Jarrow seemed fine with no indication of any stiffness.

With two days to go, fate intervened once more. I went down with one of the worst flu bugs I had in years. With head aching, nose streaming, general weakness and the shivers, I withdrew from the event twenty-four hours beforehand. As it turned out, it was a very sensible decision. But it would be a further four months before I returned to another SERC event.

As the bug cleared my head and body, I visited Jarrow daily. He seemed fine, well rested but comments from a visiting farrier caused further consternation. According to the farrier there seemed to be an early indication that some joint problems, possibly the early stages of arthritis existed. For me I had no knowledge or awareness that any previous history or pre-existing condition was discernible. But I did start to grow increasingly worried. Within a week we started training again. There was little point in any further endurance competition; instead the focus was on solitary duration work, and the need to minimise any travelling. Nevertheless, as every other day passed, alarm bells continued to rattle in my head. It was obvious that Jarrow was slowing down, his willingness to continue diminishing. He might well have had some ground behavioural issues but in his favour he had been a very competent and willing endurance horse. Now this was changing - too fast. At times he would trot on for ages but it was increasingly obvious that he was not enjoying the experience. One thing that was for certain was the fact that he was by now most definitely slowing down, enthusiasm seemingly waning as each day passed. Other times he would ride so far then simply stop, refusing to budge. Some may argue that he was in effect "napping" but that performance was not typical.

Now napping in equine speak is a most annoying habit which originates in allowing a horse to have too much of its own way. Instead of obeying, the horse tries an evasion, opposing the rider's will and often ending up by imposing its own will on the rider. A nappy horse will try every kind of avoidance to get its own way; it will suddenly stop, stand still, refuse to budge, move forward, or it will go around in circles, sidle sideways, buck or even attempt to rear up. Or it may refuse to go in the direction its rider wishes, trying every means to go the opposite way. Some horses, accustomed to going out in company will refuse to go out alone or even resist leaving the confines and security of a yard. One school of thought suggests that a rider should never give in no matter how long it takes and never dismount because the horse may construe the latter as a victory, a confession of fear or weakness by the rider. However if the horse is refusing to budge because he is being awkward, getting off and leading him will blow a hole in his strategy.

Many people have it drummed into them that if they get off, the horse has won. This is the wrong mindset, as it turns riding into a conflict. Instead, do anything – including getting off and leading – to get the horse moving in the right direction because it might just be looking for guidance or direction from the rider – it's leader. Now some will argue that forcefulness is required, even to the extent that I have seen riders thrashing their horse with a crop. In one instance a mare was baulking at a red coloured slab laid driveway. Clearly the horse was worried or confused by the coloured object. The rider's immediate thought was to lash out at a nappy horse because that's exactly what she had been taught to believe. That to me is conflict – not understanding – or oneness. Some time later, just ahead of me at a gate, a former Scottish team member's horse of veteran competition experience baulked at an earth ramp at the side of the gate. The rider's immediate reaction was to jump off, quickly lead the horse over the ramp past the gate then just as quickly remount. That was oneness and understanding – not conflict. That was thinking outside the box!

There were never any noticeable behavioural issues in getting Jarrow away from the yard, nor could we identify any tack issues that could be causing discomfort. In fact the latter had been addressed some weeks beforehand, resulting in him being fitted with a new purpose made endurance saddle. His feet were fine, bridle and bit comfortable but his actions were or seemed at least unexplained. Had Jarrow's implied napping behaviour been prevalent since the day that I had first taken him out, I would probably have been the first to concede that he was simply trying it on. But after a year of strenuous riding through forests, beaches, hill tracks and miscellaneous roads, I found that latter hypothesis too difficult to accept. Jarrow might have had some groundwork issues and could be as belligerent an animal as the next but a nappy riding horse – no. The problem lay elsewhere.

There was only one course of action that could be taken. Firstly, someone suggested that I called in an equine "physiotherapist". She in turn recommended that our vet take a closer look. A day or so later I sat on a log nearby the River Isla and listened carefully to what our vet was telling me. The diagnosis was bad, the prognosis worse. Jarrow had arthritis in three legs, the joints deteriorating. In effect his endurance days were over – today! Formerly known as degenerative joint disease (DJD), osteoarthritis is a specific form of arthritis common in horses. It can also be a permanently crippling disease. Although capable of short hacks or light work, anything longer or more demanding would simply hasten his illness, permanently cripple him. Although there was never any suggestion that on my part

I would allow this to happen I had to know then and there. In a brutally frank manner I asked the vet the stupid question that I already knew the answer to - whether Jarrow was capable of the demands that the Trans Scotland would put on him. His simple answer was all that I needed to know but didn't really want to hear. If I subjected Jarrow to those rigorous levels of endurance, I would break him. Apart from sending him down to the Royal Dick Veterinary School for a second opinion, there was nothing I could do. I was given the weekend to think about the situation. By Monday I decided that I did not want to subject the horse to a protracted stressful trailer journey and then perhaps find out just what we already knew. Jarrow's endurance career was over – now! That was the harsh reality that had to be faced.

With six weeks to go before the start date, I was shattered. I had spent nearly a year with this horse. We had some fantastic times together out in the open hills and forests, exploring the countryside. A sense of guilt hung over me – perhaps I had pushed that little bit beyond the comfort zone. Of course disappointment bit deep but I was hurting more for Jarrow, not me. When I went to see him later that day, I was glad that there was no one around. He looked over the fence at me with his big doleful eyes as much as to say – I'm sorry. In return I stroked his neck, fed him an apple and thanked him profusely for what he had done for me. As it turned out it would be the first of two occasions in the coming week that I would have to express my deepest thanks and say goodbye to my two loyal animal friends for their unconditional companionship.

The dilemma started immediately. There were only three things that could be done. I could either give up, letting the entire plan go to waste; postpone the ride for another time or find another horse and press on. It was a very difficult decision, especially after such a long period of planning and training. Therefore option one didn't really figure in the equation. Too much would have been lost. I knew perfectly well that I had one real shot at this, the opportunity never likely to come along again. Anyway, the strategy, the plan was too far advanced, too deeply embedded in my psyche to let go. There were very few people who were actually aware of what the ride was all about so backing out, or walking away wouldn't really have been too much of a dent in the ego. Similarly, I had no real responsibility to anyone other than myself to carry on, but that entire option was dismissed. On an equal basis, postponing the ride was a further alternative that had its own pitfalls. I had patiently waited for nearly a year. May was the chosen month for two reasons. Firstly we calculated that it gave us the best chance of favourable weather; secondly the anniversary of me going into hospital was due to coincide with the departure date. Furthermore, I correctly reasoned that any lengthy delay would probably result in a substantial loss of interest. If I didn't go as planned, I probably never would. If, and it was a huge IF, if I did find another horse I would be taking a massive gamble. It would be a major risk in setting off over such difficult terrain and prolonged dura-tion with an animal that I would probably only have had four weeks with. And that was assuming that I found one immediately. As it turned out with the course of events about to happen, the decision was in effect made for me.

Now fate plays funny tricks. Just over a year previously, I was acting as a Crossing Steward for a SERC event at Scone, near Perth. Stationed out at Balboughty Farm on the A93, Perth to Blairgowrie road, my task was to ensure that riders crossed the road safely, whilst trying to ensure that drivers speeding along the main road were aware that horses were crossing. It was a bitterly cold morning. Slowly then more steadily the first of the competitive riders passed through the Control Point. I noted the bib numbers, jotted down the times then went back into neutral, or nipped off for another hot drink from the Land Rover. One of first riders to pass through was Candy Cameron, ex-British Endurance Champion, winner of the Arab Marathon. As she passed by she shouted her thanks, but she was clearly engaged, her Arabian horse flowing with ease in a steady trot. I thought no more of it. Now almost a year later, this was the one person whom I turned to. If anyone could help me find a replacement horse, it was that focussed, determined looking lady who rode past my Control Point on that icy morning in March.

Although I was looking forward to the meeting with Candy, to ride the purebred Arabian that I was interested in seeing, I wasn't particularly looking forward to driving to Dores, near Inverness. The day was tinged with an overlying burden of unhappiness. I was functioning at a very low level; the commitment that had carried me along for a year was ebbing fast. Emotionally I was blank. Some external force, destiny was driving me on and nothing more. In a sense I was a mindless automaton, somehow being manipulated like a puppet. The upset in losing Jarrow was hard enough to bear but I was all too aware that this day was probably the last that I would spend with my beloved Springer Spaniel Tig. Sadly, we had realised and accepted the previous week that the tumour eating its way through him, causing him to waste away in front of us, was incurable. It was a matter of time before the pain would start and that was something that we could not even contemplate. As I drove over the hills that morning with Tig tucked up in the back of the vehicle, I prayed every minute of the journey that he would just fall asleep for one last time.

"When I cannot understand, help me to go on believing
When all seems dark, let the light of faith shine in my heart"

The time I spent with Candy at Dores was enjoyable. I badly needed some space to take my mind off the burden of guilt that haunted my inner feelings. As I trotted the flea bitten grey Arabian gelding around the indoor arena, the concentration I needed to work on what felt like a really bouncing horse kept me focussed and attentive. In fact I initially doubted the suitability simply on the basis that here was a horse of different characteristics and style, one that I was completely unused to. If Candy had any reservations, she didn't mention them. As I was to find out a little later beneath that tough exterior there really does beat a kind and warm heart; someone quick to praise - slow to criticise. But don't tell her I said that. When Candy opened up the large sliding doors to set us free into the tracks and woods above Loch Ness, I needed no further encouragement. Of course I was cautious, nervous but I felt a strange rapport with this spirited animal. I didn't believe for one minute that I could come to any harm with this horse, one that seemed to float at the trot. The sensation was remarkable. When I returned to the farm we rode up to the field overlooking the sweeping mass of Loch Ness, to drink in the glorious surroundings. In an instant I knew that quite possibly I had found my horse. Within an hour over coffee with Candy in her spacious farmhouse kitchen the deal was done.

On the way home I stopped at the old bridge near Gairnsheil for a walk. Normally Tig would have been bouncing off the inside of the Land Rover to get out into the heather. Today he just lay unmoving on his bed; still covered with the blanket I had wrapped him in. I encouraged him to get up then lifted him out into the sunshine.

Always together we walked very slowly through the heather then over the patches of snow that lay along the edge of the tumbling burn. Tig was barely able to stand; as he tried to walk he stumbled, his strength ebbing fast. I carried him to the side of the water and let him drink. We sat together for a few minutes in the bright spring afternoon listening to the occasional grouse call. I stroked his head and floppy ears and fought back the emotion. I wanted to sit with him there in the peace and quiet of the hills that he loved so much, to wait his time. Less than twenty-four hours later he was gone - peacefully and with dignity at home with me beside him.

> *"Finally when it happened*
> *I was with him at the end*
> *And I took the chance*
> *To tell him thanks*
> *For everything he had done"*

Rose and I decided to head off for a couple of days break soon after but before we left we had one heartbreaking task to perform. On one fine spring afternoon we drove into nearby Glen Lethnot. With heavy hearts we just trudged on upwards, not speaking, our thoughts our own. I took an awful lot of deep breaths to try to ease the overwhelming sense of sadness and the numbing aching pain in my heart. On that bright seasonal afternoon, the hills around us were bursting with new life but it meant nothing that day. We plodded upwards; the only sound our breathing as we gained altitude. At the gate we stopped, then looked around for a suitable spot. Rose pointed to the drystane dyke. I took out the trowel, dug a small hole then placed the poem, the photograph and his favourite toy into the soil. I covered this over with earth then placed a few stones and flowers on top. Tears flowed as we held on to each other. I took the urn then slowly, tenderly scattered Tig's ashes over the area. As if right on cue, a gentle breeze caught the dust and carried this out over the heather.

"Goodbye Tig", whispering *"Oichdhe mhath mo cu beag"*.

Beside me, Rose stood in tears.

"Goodbye Tiggy", then "He's running free now at peace"

We held each other again then sat for a while looking over the hills and glen. A peace and sudden sense of tranquillity drifted over us but a huge empty space had been left in our hearts and lives.

For a week or so my concentration, motivation lapsed. I suppose it is difficult for many people to imagine or understand what the loss of a faithful canine friend can mean but I missed the dog a huge amount. It wasn't just the loss of company but the routine, the early morning walks, and weekend strolls, nearly ten years of shooting companionship – all gone at once. With Jarrow now firmly out of the equation and Tig gone, I almost crashed into low ebb. There was every possibility that I was as close to walking away from the entire plan as I had ever been. It wasn't until I received a somewhat curt but justifiable e-mail from Candy that I snapped back into focus. Life had to move on, as much as that hurt.

Consequently, a few days later I sat in the vehicle outside the auction mart at Perth, drank more tea than was good for me and in effect spent more time than usual visiting the toilets. Time passed by slowly. I read the newspapers, visited the tack shop, browsed the clothes shops and waited. And waited. Then eventually one of Gillies' massive horse transporters rolled into the car park. As it did so a surge of unashamed boyish excitement, even apprehension washed through me. Within minutes the large unload ramp was down then out into the Perthshire countryside stepped a rather bemused looking, flea bitten grey, pure bred Arabian gelding who is still probably far too handsome for his own good. It is said in Bedouin legend that an Arabian horse finds his owner. As he followed me without hesitation into the trailer that day it seemed inevitable that my life was about to be changed all over again, turned upside down – owned by an Arabian horse. His name? Prince Omar. And in the ancient language of Kaledan Omar means *Shining Light.*

Now, according to some of the so-called equine "experts" that permeate the horse world, you either love them or hate them. Despised by the myopic attitudes of many as being too temperamental, or "fizzy" the Arabian horses probably have as large a group of antagonists as they do admirers. Much of that is probably due to ignorance with just a little smattering of sheer envy. But I did not actually give one moment's thought to any petty minded critical or hypocritical denunciations of one particular so called equine physiotherapist or the "professional" groom whose vitriolic comments were based on their own ignorance. It never ceases to amaze me how amateur, pathetic and small minded the equestrian world really is at times.

There is no horse as wonderful as the Arabian horse. Arabians are known as the only true pure bred as well as the oldest breed of equine. These horses are steeped in myth and legend as to their Bedouin origins, but even the naysayers must admit to one point, there is nothing as fabulously beautiful as the Arabian horse. Respected for their intelligence, loyalty and their beauty, the Arabian continues to captivate and inspire creating new legends to be passed down throughout the ages.

And Allah summoned the winds. From the north came Spirit, the south Strength, the east Speed and the west

Intelligence. Allah took a handful of wind, blew His breath over it, and from the four winds of the earth created the pure bred Arabian horse. He said to the magnificent creature, "I have made thee as no other. All the treasures of the earth lie between thy eyes. Happiness will hang from your forelock and no evil spirit will dare to enter where you stand. Thou shall carry my friends upon thy back. The saddle shall be the seat of prayers to me. Thou shall fly without wings, and conquer without any sword. Oh horse"

A hardy and sturdy breed, they are fine boned and elegant. The head of the Arabian stands out with short ears tipped in, large beautifully expressive eyes; a dished profile, prominent forehead and small muzzle with flared nostrils. Many Arabian horses also have a slight forehead bulge between the eyes called by the Bedouin, the *jibbah* – an apparent aid to additional sinus capacity. The tail set of the Arabian is distinctive, with the tail carried upright like a flag when the horse is excited and beautifully arched and flowing during normal movement, a symbol of pride. Arabian horses also have personality. They are fiery, inquisitive, intelligent, and affectionate and enjoy the company of people. Few hear his name without thinking of an unfettered horse, mane flowing, tail bannered in the wind, proud head held high. To be gifted with an Arabian horse is a great honour. Those of us who have the good fortune of being owned by an Arabian horse can attest that each of these characteristics, each of these legends is true. But this is a horse renowned for endurance par excellence, more than capable of out-performing any other breed over long distances. Now with only a matter of days left to go before we started off on a 200-mile sprint across Scotland, I set about bonding with a spirited son of the wind. The gamble was great, the stakes high but failure was neither considered nor an option. As Kipling would have said:

" . . . *make one heap of all your winnings. And risk it on one turn of pitch-and-toss.*"

And that is exactly what I did but in that same time as those final days passed into hours, then hours to minutes, a partnership had be forged like no other. There was everything to play for and there would be no room for error.

A matter of days later, a bright warm morning saw me load the last items of personal equipment into the Land Rover. Thankfully, I had slept well the night before. Because it as it was about to turn out, it would be the last decent nights sleep I would have for the next three days. I kissed my wife goodbye, picked up Paul and Matt then headed out to the yard. The trailer was packed ready to go, loaded with all the tack, hay, feed and spare equipment that we would need for the duration. Almost everything was doubled up. Apart from the contingencies for Nuclear, Biological, or Chemical (NBC) warfare and excluding the kitchen sink, we were almost self-sufficient. Once Omar had been unloaded our personal equipment, food, cooking equipment, water containers and clothing were transferred to the trailer – our mobile store.

Thirty minutes after Omar was fed his miniscule breakfast, we kitted him out in his travel rug, boots and tail guard. Without hesitation, bright, alert and seemingly aware that a new adventure was about to commence, he walked up the load ramp then straight into the trailer after me. Forty minutes after that, the Land Rover and trailer were inched along the narrow tarmac road that leads from the eastern end of Ferryden, outside Montrose to Scurdie Ness. At the end of the track the vehicle came to a stop just below the towering whitewashed structure that guards the entrance to the Montrose Basin.

A very slight breeze blew off the North Sea gradually dispensing the delicate haar that lay over the cold grey-blue waters. Omar was unloaded, then for a few minutes he was left to chomp hay as we sorted out his tack. Going through the checklist, I looked into those dark eyes. Are they clear and bright? Mentally tick box – clear and bright – Oh yes! Legs cold and tight? As I walked Omar around for a further short period, I introduced him to the North Sea, and then pointed out that the next ocean he would see would be the Atlantic. He did not seem too impressed.

At Scurdie Ness lighthouse there stands a commemorative cairn, which marks the finish point of The Great Outdoor Challenge. As I stood near the pillar that morning, some two hundred miles away, apparently around three hundred and ten hardy walkers were departing various points on the west coast for this location. Two hundred miles away from them, I turned Omar's rear to the North Sea behind us then headed off towards the west. No doubt somewhere our paths would converge. As we set off along the narrow tarmac road, to our right the verges dropped away quite sharply to the narrow channel leading from the North Sea into Montrose harbour and basin. Beyond the industrialism of the town, the hills could be seen, almost shimmering in the mid morning sun. I gave out a solitary whoop of delight as finally we were on our way. Omar's ears pricked up. We marched on towards Ferryden, the traffic, twisting roads then eventually the open countryside. Ahead of us lay two hundred odd miles of roads, rivers, precipitous mountain trails, open moorland and forest tracks. What also lay ahead of us was some of the most dangerous, inhospitable and isolated terrain in Britain. There would be no indicator tapes, no talk-arounds, and no biogradable spray paint markings to show the way. If I sensed any hint of apprehension, it must have been minimal. As the stopwatches started the merciless countdown then reversed to count back up we stepped forward over the line. Let battle commence!

The tedium of roads from Montrose soon passed, traffic declined as we climbed up from the flat coastal plains of Angus. We stopped for a quick lunch at a picnic site and small car park that lies to the north of Brechin overlooking the Vale of Strathmore. The stopping point was as much practical as it was symbolic. On the crest of the high ground we could look back to see the North Sea shimmering in the distance at Montrose, the white painted lighthouse at Scurdie Ness standing like a proud sentinel, guarding the entrance to Montrose basin. Ahead lay the prominent rising ground and valley that represented the entrance into the hills, the southern portion of the Cairngorm National Park. Behind us now lay the starting point, ahead was the challenge of the mountains. The air was still, the sky cloudless, the day growing warmer as the sun rose higher. From the vantage point overlooking the surrounding countryside we prepared for the steady steep descent that would take us gradually down from nearly a thousand feet towards Blairno.

On each side of the road that leads down into Glen Lethnot there stands the remains of the ancient Pictish hill top settlements or forts known as the Brown and White Caterthuns. Their names actually refer to the different forms of construction, which in turn suggest two different dates of occupation. The Brown Caterthun comprises of five or six concentric earth banks. These banks were originally made of turf, laid over stone and can be seen as a series of raised lines under the heather. The Brown Caterthun may have been constructed as a defensive or ritual structure and likely to been formed between 3000 BC and 300 BC. It is suggested that the Brown Caterthun was already out of use when the White Caterthun was constructed, probably by the Picts when they arrived in the area in the first centuries AD; and so it could possibly have seen active service when Agricola's highly disciplined Roman legion marched past en route to their victory at Mons Graupius in AD84.

The White Caterthun comprises a massive oval stone rampart around the top of the hill at a height of 298 metres. It is clearly marked by a broad band of stones following the line of the original rampart. Within the circle of stones at the summit, their lies a stone filled pit, presumably used as a quarry or well. Both the Brown and White Caterthuns command spectacular views in all directions.

With each steady footstep, every burst of trotting, we gradually left the fertile sweep of the low-lying Angus countryside and civilisation behind us. From the Caterthuns we descended the steep road that took us into Glen Lethnot. Spring was receding fast, the roadside now flanked by green fields edged with yellow bursting gorse The hills stood out clearly in the blue skies of a warm afternoon sun, colours developing throughout the heather as spring passed into early summer. Patches of "muir" burn, indicators of some serious, well-established yet artificial grouse moor management were evident against the myriad of shades generated by the young heather and greens of bracken. It was a hot day with little air but the ride despite being the brain numbing tedium of endless roadwork was pleasant enough to tune muscles for the more strenuous days ahead. Now relieved to be away from the strains of traffic, I started to relax. The Land Rover and trailer buzzed head, opening gates at the cattle grids, forewarning traffic that we were coming.

For a short time we stopped near the road across from Craig of Finnoch for some hurried re-hydration. On the east side of the glen, the high stone cairns apparently marking the graves of ancient suicides stood out clearly along the ridge like large mannequins, corpses buried in un-conse-crated ground. Even in the warm air I shivered at the thought. As I looked high up onto the side of Craig Duch-ray's sweeping hillside, I thought about Tig wondering if the flowers were still there. Then I thought of other times, remembering the run from the storm with Jarrow. How different the weather was now. How much had happened over those last few weeks and months. The wounds were still painful but my mind was firmly switched back to the task in hand. It was a beautiful day. There was neither room nor need for sadness. It was time to be away from there. We carried on, walking and trotting for the last few miles, clattered over the narrow hump back bridge at Stoneyford, crossing the West Water, then swung on to a final heading that brought us to our first staging point and overnight stop.

We reached Hunthill Lodge in reasonable time, fenced off the paddock for Omar then Paul and Matt headed home to Brechin for the night. Feeling just a tad lonesome I was left at the bothy, provided by Dave Donley, the Hunthill Estate Head Gamekeeper. The red brick building that housed the bothy accommodation for the young trainee gamekeepers was comfortable, well equipped. From the rear window I looked straight out to Omar's paddock. He in turn spent a lot of the time looking into the window at me.

By the time I finished my evening meal the sky remained crystal clear. I spent a tranquil half hour sipping my mug of tea, admiring the surrounding terrain. Seated on the load ramp of the trailer parked beside the paddock the peaceful-ness of the glen was soothing. The only sound was the West

Water that gurgled at the foot of the field below the kennels or the occasional cuckoo call. I fussed around for a while sorting out the tack for next day, not really sure if I had to or if it was just an exercise to keep me occupied before bedtime. I was fully aware that tomorrow would be the first very real test to come for this partnership but didn't dwell on the matter even though for the most part of the day we would be isolated, out of radio and mobile telecommunications range.

As a matter of curiosity, I switched on my handheld GPS if only to see how long it would take for the signal to stabilise. Within a few minutes a full complement of SVs had locked into the system to provide a position to +/- 10 metres. Knowing that we had stopped a few hundred metres short of the end of the first stage, curiosity led me on to have a quick look at the slight distance addition to the route. Flicking the mini joystick through the GPS pages I seemed to be unable to locate Route 2A, which was the three thousand odd feet climb from Hunthill up over the Goet then the tricky, perilous descent down into Glen Clova that followed.

It didn't really take too long to realise that a technical problem somewhere had resulted in that one route not being downloaded from the PC. Although I did have a print out of the co-ordinates for every waypoint along each route, the paperwork was in the vehicle, which in turn was twenty odd miles away. Even so, it would have taken half the night to reprogram the unit by manual input. Anyway, I had a series of good scale maps and my trusty compass. Nonetheless I did sincerely hope that the cloud base would stay high, maintaining good visibility. So on that happy note - off to bed I went.

Sleep evaded me. The constant thrum from a nearby freezer kept me awake half the night. The more I concentrated on trying to sleep the more I focussed on the infernal irritating hum of the domestic machine. Getting tenser as each minute passed, I was tempted to switch off the unit, but knew that the food stash lying within the icy compartment belonged to the trainee gamekeeper next-door. He probably would not have thanked me for defrosting his pies and frozen vegetables even though I would have been long gone before he discovered the damage. Of course there is no point in trying to sleep when sleeplessness ensures that it has become impossible. I got up, wandered around the room, looked out into the darkness to see if I could spot Omar then made a mug of tea. Eventually I dozed off into a fitful sleep where a buzzing fridge freezer monster stalked my every hour. Dawn broke too quickly. By 5am, as light poured into the windows of my bed-sit type room. I was wide-awake. Bleary eyed I made a leisurely mug of tea, then shaved, showered and quickly threw a basic breakfast into me. Too nervous to eat much I knew that a long day ahead of me demanded some form of sensible nourishment. Omar was fed, watered and groomed before my belongings were packed up.

By seven I was ready, itching to go. Paul and Matt turned up right on cue. Then nerves started to take over. I wanted to be on my way before the tension could eat deeper. With Omar tacked, I heaved the heavily laden bum bag containing the maps, functioning GPS but without the route for the day, food, water bottles, first aid kit and various other items around me before setting off past the lodge towards the start of the track at Waterhead. It was a stunningly beautiful morning. The skies were azure blue, absolutely crystal clear, the hills standing out, shimmering in multi colours. Already the sun was throwing its heat on to us – it was going to be a very hot day. I reached forward and took Omar's muzzle in my hands. I gently kissed his nose. Then in true Rocky style,

"No fear. No pain", I whispered. Then climbed into the saddle.

For a moment I sat relaxed, feeling the warm morning sun on my back. I took a deep breath, closed my eyes then squeezed my left thumb with my right fingers. For ten seconds I was gone, completely detached in relaxation. Apparently, Arthur Ash and Billy Jean King, the champion tennis players were early practitioners of active visualisation in sport, the ability to close one's eyes and withdraw for a moment. For this to be effective you must not just "leave" the location but also actually "arrive" somewhere else – an imagined place where you are alone and relaxed. Squeezing my thumb was the trigger needed start the process, to conjure up the imagined place of relaxation and at the same time silently recite three lines of an ancient prayer. It was the last little bit of team spirit, turning my attention and energy away from myself and towards the common objective. As it was about to transpire, that common objective would keep me physically and psychologically focussed for the next few days.

Dave Donley had warned me that a helicopter would be airlifting fencing equipment out to the marches but expected that I would be well on my way by the time it arrived. Thankfully I was. The idea of being buzzed in the confines of the glen was not a particular scenario that I considered to be a bundle of fun. At the makeshift heli-pad, I bobbed and weaved Omar through the stacks of posts, coils of wire and related transport equipment that was stockpiled at the first gate. The estate was in the process of fencing off the entire boundary in order to better control the red deer population and hence encourage more optimistic approaches to grouse development. It is a strategy that is being adopted by a number of estates throughout Scotland and in particular the southern portion of the Grampians. Whether it is a strategy that will work is highly debateable. Only time will provide the real indicators as to whether this form of conservation will be effective in re-establishing the grouse as a viable sporting commodity.

I glanced back once to wave to Paul then turned my attention to the task in hand - ahead of us some three thousand feet of steady climbing and nearly twenty kilometres to the first crew point. At least for the first two kilometres or so, the track into the glen was flat, solid, following close to the edge of the tumbling West Water. We made good speed but in a leisurely manner to let muscles warm up. As we neared the start of the strenuous hill path that the estate workers call the zigzag, I slowed Omar into a walk. Briefly, I scanned the track ahead; for all intents and purposes there was a similarity to this being a mini version of the Devil's Staircase as it twisted, snaked its way up the hillside. It also looked perilously smooth, rocky and steep. Ironically, this track had been originally built for the hill ponies that carried panniers for grouse shooting parties or for extracting deer from the distant hill. I could just imagine the heavy sure-footed garrons, our native Highland ponies shuffling their way along these tracks. As we approached the start, I brought Omar to a halt, took a deep breath, shortened reins, balanced myself in the stirrups, and squeezed my lower legs against the horse's side. Then we were off.

Highland Cathedral

"Do not go where there is a trail but instead leave a path to follow."

T HERE were really only two ways to approach the climb. The first was to take it easy as a slow steady boring upward plod. The second option was to let Omar run. I lined up on the middle of the lower section, lifted myself just slightly out of the saddle then started the climb at speed. Completely at ease, Omar powered up over the smooth rock, evidently exposed where the original surface had been obliterated by water run off. We climbed higher, faster, sweeping around the twisting turns. My mind was completely focussed. The only sound the clatter of hoofs over the smooth flat rocky sections, Omar's steady breathing. It was an exhilarating ride over a gradient that seemed almost vertical in places.

Soon we were high above the glen. I looked back and down in awe at the valley far below us, the West Water now a thin sliver of glinting light. In the distance the thump thump of the rotors could be heard as the helicopter came in for its first lift. We kicked on to the plateau, over the wet rocky path that lay at nearly two thousand feet above sea level. Waterhead faded into the distance. Ahead lay only the silence and solitude of a sweeping mass of heather clad hillside. Girls Aloud sprung to mind. The song that is! I think!

*I think we're alone now. There doesn't seem to be
anyone around.
I think we're alone now. The beating of our hearts
is the only sound*

For a few minutes we slowed to cool down. Despite the
early hour of the morning, the sun was pouring heat onto
us. Even at this altitude there was little wind. Sweat
dribbled out from under my riding helmet. For a short
distance the ground was churned up with a pitfall of sharp
loose stones scattered amidst the soft sandy sections. We
walked slowly, very, very carefully through this section of
loose spongy earth until we reached the first cascading ford,
the firmness of harder ground beyond then the gradual
descent to run parallel with the tumbling stream.

In a sense I suppose that Omar came as a ready-made
endurance package. For he is a grandson of the legendary
Sky Crusader, the highly successful Arabian flat racer
whose genes passed on to numerous triumphant American
competitive endurance horses. Omar also came with attitude, not issues. He may well have inherited some of his
grandmother's flat speed but he could climb – the steeper
and hotter the better. His background was stable but a freak
accident left his original owner unable to cope with the
demands of an Arabian gelding. From there he passed into
the more than capable hands of Candy Cameron where he
was "re-educated" as an endurance horse. Omar typically
excelled at the sport gaining a SERC Bronze Thistle in a
short time and indeed performing well in Le Trec where he
was only beaten by his stable mate Louistic de Tunes. From
there, he passed on to me, ready, conditioned and more
than prepared to increase competitive distances. It wouldn't

be too long before we would knock the cotton socks off
those early times and speeds.

"From sire to sire, it's born in the blood
The fire of a mare and the strength of a stud
It's breeding and it's training
But it's something unknown
That drives you to carry you home"

But for the moment there I was, at nearly two thousand
feet above sea level with nothing ahead or around me but
open hillside and isolation, sitting atop the Arabian horse
that I had owned for just over four weeks. No doubt to
many, at that moment in time I was punching way above
my weight. But at least I was still punching! As someone
once described our partnership, Omar and I "came together
in a strange arrangement where we meet each other toe-to-
toe, eye-to-eye and neither will back off. Lacking the finesse
of the refined, polished pugilist, this is a pair of unpredict-
able street fighters that are liable to kick or gouge at any
moment without warning and whose simplistic approach
is a head down, bring it on and we will slug it out together
as a partnership from start to finish attitude." With that in
mind, we moved on - together.

"C'mon Omar, lets trot on a bit."

Snort!

For the next four miles, we rode along the precarious
edge of the hillside named Horse Holm, through mud,
heather, splashed over fords, gradually descending into the
head of the glen. Almost level with us, The Shank of Donald
Young passed on the left. It was here in the 1600s that a
bloody battle took place at the top of the Glen called "The
battle of the Saughs". It was between young Cateranians
(Lethnot) and 18 men from Fern. The battle was fought over

cattle and horse rustling issues. The Shank of Donald Young marks the spot where Donald Young, from Glen Lethnot, was killed by the sword. Many Glen Lethnot men were injured during the battle, and a few were mortally wounded. The "Fern Men" returned home victorious with only one lost. Just below where the Burn of Duskintry meets the Water of Saughs there is a swinging suspension footbridge that leads to the path over the Shank. Just beyond that a tumbling waterfall carves its way down the rocky hillside to end in a deep silent pool. In the past I had heard of too many tales of encounters with ghostly voices on that side of the hill near the waterfall. So we didn't linger. In the distance another piece of history was waiting - the old Shieling of Saughs – our first target point for the day.

According to John Burnett, writing in the Angry Corrie, the Shieling of Saughs is possibly the highest house above sea level to have been inhabited all year round. This is the distinction that exists between a shieling and a bothy whereby the latter would be occupied intermittently rather being linked to seasonal grazing. This particular shieling stands at 630m in a remote spot near the head of the Water of Saughs. It is both the site of a high shieling (based on its name) and a very high house. People who came to graze cattle on ground remote from their winter quarters so that the lowland grass could recover over the summer inhabited these places during the season. Shielings were usually chosen well above the winter *toun*. Under the name *tran-shumance* this practice has been identified over much of Europe, as when the Swiss take their cattle to the Alps. The shieling is small but stands with a roof and three walls still intact. In its time, it must have been an interesting place to live.

At the isolated ruin I dismounted, led Omar to the crystal clear water of the burn to drink, then I munched on a fruit flavoured porridge bar, washing it down with a topped up water supply from the stream. Omar searched around for some grassy morsel but soon decided that the oaty bar in my hand offered a better proposition. He keenly jostled me for a position that would strategically place his face within distance of my mouth but was even more disappointed when I placed the half eaten section back into my pocket. The girth was checked, a couple of adjustments made to the tack then we set off again. The total stoppage time was less than five minutes. From the shieling, we crossed the flowing water at the ford then started the long laborious ascent to the summit of The Goet. For the first part, the track, a solid Land Rover road lay directly ahead but incredulously it was completely blocked by deep snow for about thirty feet over its length, each side of the track rising sharply to steep heather banks. My search for an alternative was quickly discounted as there was no way around the obstacle.

Inevitably we had to cross the bank of snow. Omar was nudged on but resisted. I turned him in the tight space then tried again. He placed one foot tentatively into the soft cold white stuff but didn't like it. Obviously, the regal desert genes were not programmed for this. Omar likes familiar things. He doesn't like cold soft stuff that squelches or crunches underfoot. He hesitated again. But I was losing patience – fast. I coaxed him on. He stepped into the snow. Good boy! Now a bit further! As I reached towards his neck for a pat of encouragement, his feet crashed through the inches of hard layered snow to touch the firm ground below. Unexpectedly he bunny hopped forward. Unprepared, we parted company. I lay back in the welcome coldness of the snow – bliss! Omar now clear of the snow barrier in three rather lengthy strides stood perfectly still waiting for me. His look of utter dismay and distaste was blatantly obvious

– as much as to say what are you waiting for? We have work to do! Snooty Arab!

We pushed on upwards. As we cleared the heather clad hillside, frequently dotted with well-maintained grouse butts, the track ceased. The heather gave way to patches of sparse grass surrounded by inky black peat hags. The landscape was monotonous; the mountain grasses bleached with a more greyish brown shade that dominated the sweeping ground. A mountain hare, almost clear of its white winter coat, darted out ahead of us. Somewhere in the distance a grouse called out.

"Go back, go back, go back"

"Walk on Omar", I coaxed defiantly in reply.

Snort!

As we worked our way up Black Shank, the helicopter clattered overhead, giving us a generous wide berth. In the distance fencing dumps with the marker posts, red and white tape fluttering in the light breeze were clear against the skyline. We dropped down into a hollow before starting the steady ascent of The Goet. The ground, covered in the sparse mountain grass typical of this altitude was hard. There was no evident path, no tell tale marker tapes but we pushed on. I reached for my map holder and compass to check the bearing then discovered that my trusty orienteering compass was gone, lost somewhere back in the distance. Impatient now, I wanted to drive on. Undeterred, a mental calculation with a crude bearing from the surrounding tops was sufficient to show the way. A faint section of path allowed us to actually trot right up to, and beyond the summit triangulation pillar.

At the summit of The Goet, we rode past the rocky cairn and triangulation pillar to look straight down into the inky black waters of Loch Wharral, a thousand feet below. Seconds later we stepped over the imaginary line that demarcates the boundary of the Cairngorms National Park. The scenery was spectacular. I could see the length of Glen Lethnot behind me, Mount Keen in the distance, Lochnagar and the White Mounth visible to the north. Below us the trees and plain of Glen Clova were bathed in glorious sunshine. The South Esk shimmered in the heat. Isolation was obvious. There was no sound. Eternally grateful that we were basking in glorious clear and remarkably dry conditions I rightly envisaged that this would not have been a place to loiter in low cloud or poor visibility. I pulled out the UHF radio then sent out the pre-arranged morse-code signal.

Beep – Beep – Beep. Dash – Dash – Dash.

The acknowledgement response came back in seconds. Marc was on location at the first crew point at Wheen some 1800 feet below us.

The weather was astonishing. In the shelter of the hills it was baking hot. Not only was I in direct sunshine for most of the morning but I had also been sitting on top of 300 plus kilos of living radiator that gave out a steady heat from a body that runs on a normal temperature level of 38 degrees Centigrade or 100.4 degrees Fahrenheit. The harder a horse works, the more heat it produces. Yet Omar stayed reasonably cool, his light coat amply reflecting the heat, the black skin below preventing any burn. The only real perspiration on him was from me! But the heat generated from the horse, the close contact to the equine body shedding excess warmth and consistent weight loss, was added to the exposure of an increasingly higher ambient temperature as the day wore on. I was hot! Thirsty! Sweat lashed off me, soaking my clothes. Unknown to me as the perspiration ran down my back, the heavy bum bag was gradually causing a friction burn at the bottom of my spine. Slowly stripping off the skin over a large area in readiness for a massive blister, the airflow panels slid unhindered up and down over my thin clothing. In the past hour I had consumed more than one litre of water and one electrolyte re-hydration pack. But even so thirst was a problem, dehydration was gradually starting to kick in.

It is an insidious enemy. Without observation or awareness dehydration can sneak up too quickly. Symptoms generally become noticeable after 2% of a person's normal water volume has been lost. Not particularly worried but I knew from times in the desert that vigilance was necessary. Even in the temperate climate of the UK, a person can loose as much as 2.5 litres of water, reducing endurance levels by as much as 30%. Exposed as I was to a hot day such as this, combined with strenuous exercise the fluid loss would be much greater. Apart from a slightly sore head, there were no noticeable symptoms. I felt no onset of fatigue, in fact quite the opposite. But I drunk as much liquid as I could without overdoing the intake levels, supplementing the water with electrolyte gel. Drink plenty before, during and after – the basic rule of thumb.

The descent was difficult but thankfully the conditions were dry and firm. The way led over the nutrient poor mat grass *nardus stricta* that predominates at this altitude, circumventing the edge of peat hags where the blanket bog has eroded This was infertile moorland and heath right on the edge of the arctic-alpine zone. For the most part the vegetation is heather interspersed with an abundance of plants that can survive at these altitudes. These include sedge, bog asphodel, cotton grass, purple moor grass and cross-leaved heath. For someone with the time, it is a naturalist's heaven. For me, the colours and structure of the plant life meant the difference between good solid ground and a potential trap. According to the map the path that I could see bent away to the northwest but my reasoning told me of course that couldn't be right. I pulled out my route card, took a crude bearing with my watch dial towards a point where I calculated the proper track should be then followed my instinct. It was a steep steady descent, a painfully slow one step at a time but unhurriedly; carefully we descended by contouring the hillside. We moved away from soft hummock to solid ground ever watchful for the bright green mosses and flushes of *Sphagnum* a step into which could see us go belly deep in a quagmire. But each step took us that little bit closer to success.

Below us, at the south end of Loch Wharral, a group of hill-walkers looked up in amazement at the light grey horse and fluorescent clad rider picking their way down through the heather clad hillside. I took a further bearing from their position at the end of the loch, projected that back over the contour. Spot on! Within in few minutes I picked up the bare outline of a path then followed this. Minutes later we reached the established, well-worn track that would lead us down almost a thousand feet in just over a kilometre to the north end of the Adielinn Plantation. Sweat trickled off me again as the heat from the sun joined the sweltering stagnant air in the sheltered glen. Now on solid ground we picked our way down the rocky path through the lower sections of moorland, increasing speed. Here the landscape was lacklustre, the open heath is artificial, maintained by burning, sheep grazing and tree pulling. The path was well worn, trampled by the boots of hill walkers climbing to the Wharral coire and now by a light grey Arabian horse.

I called Marc on the radio. He would be waiting at the gate near the woods for us. After a slow steady walk downhill over the narrow track that alternated with rock, mud and hard earth we closed on the edge of the plantation. We stopped with him long enough to cool down, rested for a few minutes then continued downhill through the wet boggy ground buzzing with insect life before reaching the end of the plantation and the narrow road that runs along Glen Clova. From Wheen we had a comparatively easy ride along the glen for a further six miles to our next crew point. Traffic was quiet, drivers remarkably considerate. After the strain of the last couple of hours, it was relaxing to ride easily through the glen. Apart from Omar being startled by a solitary pheasant squawking its way out of the undergrowth at the side of the road, nothing of significance happened. Above us to the right, rock climbers prepared for the ascent of Monster Crack on Red Craig. At the Doonie, I glanced upwards to Vindaloo, the route I had made the first ascent of so many years ago. On the left, dominating the glen Dreish reared its bulk in almost alpine dimensions. It was the first real opportunity to drink in the relaxing surroundings but there was no time to loiter.

Crew Point 2 was the Forest Enterprise car park at the head of Glen Clova where walkers and tourists busied around fascinated by the grey horse. Bystanders watched amazed as we breezed in, were quickly replenished then moved out. It was a seemingly well-disciplined routine. Omar was fed an oral jab of electrolytes to help reduce the risk of dehydration, encourage him to drink more. I munched a section of my energy bar, replenished my water supply, and squeezed the distasteful, but necessary electrolyte gel for humans, into my own mouth. We then headed off along the well-worn track to Moulzie towards the start of the Capel Mounth, the old drove road that would take us over the hill to the next stage point at Loch Muick. Interestingly, as we went through the gate on the east bank of the Southesk River we would be entering Balmoral the first of the only four estates that covered the next 60 miles. The green and white painted sign showed the way:

Heading for the hills

The first climb ahead of us

The Goet behind us now

Capel Mounth on the right

Isolation seems obvious

Paul crewing at 2,000 ft

Matt and the tarpaulin bridge

Mar Lodge

Out of Pennant's horrible glen

At Blair Castle

Roadwork to Rannoch

Rannoch Moor

Removing the damaged shoe

Re-shoeing at Killiecrankie

The next time - I'll read the map

Above Kinlochleven

Vet treatment at Fort William

Mingary, Ardnamurchan Peninsula

Leaving Kilchoan

End of the road

Going home

30 kms to go!

Out in the heat

PUBLIC FOOTPATH TO BALLATER
BY CAPEL MOUNTH

Marc walked with us through the lower section of the forest until we passed through the old metal gate that lies just before the Capel Burn. It is a particularly nasty little stream a steep bank on the other side and with poor footing for a skinny-legged horse with small feet. It gave me some concern when I had walked up the path earlier in the year but I suppose I had simply placed a "rider obstacle" in the way. But when the moment counts it was a case of looking straight ahead as we splashed through the cold tumbling water without hesitation. I should have known better. We then bid our goodbyes to Marc with a "see you at Blair Atholl", and then set off at speed up the twisting, winding track.

Omar powered up the climbs, over the rocky surface without a let up. Within minutes we had negotiated the final turn around the fallen timber at the old fence then were clear of the trees. The open hillside with its narrow winding track lay ahead. Well above the tree line, I looked back down to Glen Clova with a sigh of relief. The car park was receding into the distance. For the next half an hour we edged along the narrow precipitous path, twisting and winding over the route that contoured the hillside. The Capel Burn with its waters crashing over numerous small waterfalls now lay to our right, a few hundred feet below us. The mud and rock gave way to a softer mat grass covered footing, the track gradually opening out as the altitude increased steadily with each step. We turned a further corner and the summit was suddenly there. With only six kilometres to go on undulating yet firm track the hardest part of the day was very firmly behind us. I started to relax even more.

In the Scottish Mountaineering handbook, "The Cairngorms", it is stated that the Capel Mounth possibly derives its name from the Gaelic - Mounth of Horses. This is largely incorrect in that the nearest Gaelic translation would be "capull" – a mare, horses being "eich". It is more likely that the term originates from "capella" – a chapel, the explanation to this lies at the Spital of Muick some six miles over the hill from Glen Clova. It is not far from the easterly shore of Loch Muick that the Bishop of Aberdeen once established a hospice, which would have had its own chapel. It is also recorded that the hospice near the Spital was below an alehouse. Neither of these are clearly evident today. All that is left are some piles of stones although the original key to the hospice is on display at the Spital of Muick Visitor Centre. A great heavy forged iron implement, the dimension of the key suggests that its lock guarded an entrance of sizable proportions.

The Capel Mounth was used as a drove road and for harvesters, "thravers" to cross into the more fertile glens of Angus. It is also the route that Lord Ogilvy's Forfarshire Regiment retreated northwards towards Culloden on the 12 ʰ February 1746. Pursued by avenging government forces, the battle weary soldiers eventually took a stand on a water soaked moor some four miles east of Inverness. What happened on that fateful day at Drumossie has long since been consigned to the chronicles of history, the consequences of an alternative outcome debated intensely. Had the right flank held their ground for just a few more minutes against the murderous enfilade or the centre had been better supported it is likely that the Government forces would have fled the field in defeat. But at the end of the day some 1200 rebel troops and 300 odd Government forces lay dead. Then the butchery and social injustices followed. That should remain indelibly embedded in the British psyche as a constant reminder of the disgraces perpetrated against its own population and humanity. After the misfortunes of that last pitched battle fought on British soil on the 16 ʰ April 1746, it was over this same hill that the tattered remnants of the broken Regiment returned to be disbanded at the old kirk near Milton of Clova. Over the centuries, Jacobites, drovers, harvesters, travellers have all crossed this time worn track. Nowadays, the route is a popular well-marked and easy thoroughfare for hill-walkers and mountain cyclists. Oh! And one more rebel on a light grey Arabian horse.

The many small cairns erected as markers for travellers who ventured over the route in poor or winter conditions undoubtedly identify makeshift memorials to those who lost their lives crossing the openness of this sweeping stretch of moorland. It was close to one such cairn that I jumped off to take what our American cousins would call a "comfort break." On a more basic level it also afforded the opportunity to check the urine sample for dehydration. My glucose burn rate also seemed to be in pretty good shape. Then I sat back for a few minutes to bask in the warm afternoon. Lulled by the silence and stillness, sleep almost took over. A pint of ice-cold lager floated before me. Omar chomped at some grass, then with ears standing in focussed alertness diverted his attention over to the slopes of the Dog Hillock that lay directly north west of us. A large herd of red deer grazed their way along the southern slope as Omar; ears in attentive posture, watched their every move. There was no sound. I was again surrounded by the quiet solitude and sanctity of wide-open mountain spaces, holy places. I sat perfectly still for a few minutes, squeezed my left thumb with my right hand and let my mind relax.

*"Remove from my mind all distractions, inattention, coldness
Open my eyes to see you, my ears to hear you
Help me to be still in your presence."*

My eyes started to close, my mind drifting into restfulness; the tranquillity eased me into perfect peace. There was no noise, no sound yet the silence seemed to have music of its own. The warm sun soothed my face. My muscles relaxed, my breathing steadied, deepened then slowed. My eyes grew heavy as slowly I sank into a serene state. Sleep or lack of it was catching up. I was a nanosecond away from slumber but Omar shuffled around impatiently at the end of the reins, snapping me alert. It was time to go before I really did fall asleep. I pressed the pre-arranged call sign on the UHF radio then moved on.

Seconds later the signal came back in response. The electronic beeps seemed to echo for miles. We moved off quickly, steadily, trotting on the good solid track that rises and falls over the side of Gallow Hillock. Omar stopped to drink at every ford we crossed but I encouraged that indulgence. It had been a long hot day. As we climbed over a further rise, I spotted two figures in the distance. Paul and Matt had walked up part of the way from the Spital to meet us. When we joined up, Matt handed me a welcome mug of coffee from the flask. For a while, we stood gazing out over the remarkable scenery around us. To the north the snow capped coire of Lochnagar was clearly in view. The deep heather clad hillside from Cuidhe Crom sweeping steeply down to the shore of Loch Muick, its waters glinting in the afternoon sun. Further west the tip of the Central Slabs of Creagan Dubh Loch was just visible. Ahead of us on each side of the track red deer grazed, the stags now without antlers but still identifiable by their deep, thick hair covered chests Together we walked the last couple of kilometres to the Spital of Muick where the support vehicle, trailer and our makeshift accommodation for the night was in readiness next to Fiona Smith, the Balmoral Ranger's house. Tired but pleased that the first real testing day was firmly over; we went through the routine with Omar. The horse was fed, watered and groomed. The last remnants of his winter coat that grew over his rump came out in handfuls to leave a smooth glossy surface. Fiona reckoned that the hairs drifting off in the light breeze would be ideal nesting material for the plethora of bird life that bred around the area. Regal recycling at its best!

Paul and Matt had fenced off a paddock to the rear of the woods but we soon discovered that this was very quickly populated by red deer stags who cunningly dipped under the top strand of electric fencing tape. We rectified the matter by chasing them out then running a middle strand. Omar could at least get some peace for the night. The glass of cold lager that I had hallucinated over a couple of hours previously, very quickly lost its attraction as the sun sank over the White Mounth. As darkness fell the chill of the night at nearly fourteen hundred feet above sea level slowly crept in. With it, I crawled into my sleeping bag on top of the hay bales thinking that surely tonight I would be sufficiently tired enough to get a good nights sleep.

To suggest that I slept well that night on top of the hay bales within the trailer would be a gross misrepresentation of fact. The heavy load in my bum bag had caused a very serious friction burn to the small of my back; constant climbing and descending had produced a massive blister right down the base of my spine. This made sleeping very difficult. For a few minutes I lay on top of my sleeping bag on the hay bales and propped my legs over the breast bar in an attempt to drain any lactic acid off my legs. The activity was abandoned very quickly as the blister burned through me. Sleeping with my head pointed down the slope was less appealing. It also turned into a warm night, uncomfortably hot in the confines of the trailer. For most of the night I tossed and turned, too warm to need any benefit from being cocooned in a sleeping bag capable of withstanding temperatures of down to –15 degrees. Each time I turned and did drop off, I awoke with a mouthful of hay. If I turned on to my back, the roughness of my bed chafed at the worsening blister at the base of my spine. The deep-pitched hum originating from the tent next door reverberated through the thin walls of the trailer and drove me to distraction. Paul blamed Matt for snoring. Matt blamed Paul. I blamed them both. So in true sense of adventurous spirit, I rose to the challenge – I suffered in silence. But to rest is not to conquer, onwards and upwards etc, etc, blah, blah! Bleary eyed, exhausted and in pain from a very sore blistered back, boy was I glad to see morning.

In the absence of any alternative facilities, we used the public toilets at the Spittal car park for our ablutions. There was no hot water, so I made do with cleaning my teeth then splashed cold water over my head and face. I felt rough. And I looked it. Mind you most people will say I always look rough. It is quite amazing, amusing just how quickly someone can be stereotyped from facial features. As Lauren Bacall said, although I have to confess it wasn't to me personally, *"I think your whole life shows in your face, and you should be proud of that"*.

So there!

Breakfast comprised of coffee and a Stoats Porridge bar. Tony Stone, one of the Stoats company directors had given me a donation of a couple of cases of their produce for the ride. The high-energy bars were a godsend. The company started in Edinburgh in 2005 with a small trailer selling fresh flavoured organic porridge. Their signature Cranachan flavoured porridge soon gained a reputation with "in the know" foodies, sufficiently so for the company to be selected as a best European food stall by the Guardian and Herald newspapers. Using only the best Scottish organic oats, the high energy-source bars are packed with natural ingredients making them particularly ideal for anyone engaged in sporting endurance activities. With the raspberry and honey flavoured bar inside me, the high levels of antioxidants and slow energy burn would be quite sufficient to keep me alert for the next couple of hours. It may have been decidedly hypocritical of me; maybe I should have felt just the slightest hint of guilt but the utmost craving for a big fat juicy bacon roll stayed with me for a good while!!

Before I had settled into the saddle, boots comfortable in the stirrups Omar displayed his sense of impatience, ready to be off. I turned him away from the vehicle, stopping long enough to agree a meeting time with Fiona then set off through the gate. Needing no further encouragement, we trotted off easily then turned right and slightly downhill towards the Lochnagar path. We clattered over the wooden bridge that spans the River Muick then swung right into the trees near to the Alt-na-Giubhsaich cottage, now used as accommodation by the University of Aberdeen climbing club who had "kindly" refused us permission to use the accommodation for the night.

Originally we had the benefit of two options for the route between the Spital of Muick and Balmoral. These had been passed on to Glynn Jones, the Balmoral Ranger who in turn suggested that we follow the marginally longer but better track from the north of Inchnabobart to the gates at Buailteach near the Royal Lochnagar Distillery. The slightly shorter route involved a section of very rough track that led through the curious defile known as Clais Rathadan towards the shoulder of the Meikle Pap and the footpath to the summits of Lochnagar. Its not a particularly steep route but it is very narrow with a pitfall of rock and boulder strewn along its lower sections. It would have been mind numbingly slow progress, the terrain not particularly suited for a skinny-legged Arabian. Realistically anything gained in the shorter distance would have been reduced through the slow speed of progress. Therefore it made more sense to take the longer but much smoother track. It was a sensible choice.

At the Alt-na-Giubhsaich we branched right then followed a well-constructed track along the edge of the mature pine plantation. It was another beautiful day but for the first time clouds were gathering to the north-west as we joined the track carving its way through the forest before joining a further road just north west of Inchnabobart. A brightly painted sign reminded me that there were locked gates four miles ahead.

Inchnabobart was once the site of an alehouse, no doubt a scheduled stopping off point for the travellers and drovers that made their way from Deeside through Strath Girnock. The hospices were succeeded in many places by hostelries and this is what happened at Glen Muick during the early part of the last century. The Spital inn, which stood near the banks of the Alt Darrarie, succeeded an earlier inn near the ford at Inchnabobart and remained in business until the middle of the century. According to Robert Smith, author of Grampian Ways, the Inchnabobart inn, possibly one of the highest in altitude recorded in Scotland, was known as the "teetabootie" which meant, "Look about you". What the drovers or travellers were being invited to look at is anyone's guess. Perhaps brigands, ghosts or ghouls roamed the hills ready to prey on inattentive passers-by. Just in case I had a good look around me as we moved into the forest, my hand reaching for the handle of my riding crop, securely clipped onto my bum bag. Catch me if you can!!

We passed through the trees then into the open hillside and moorland with the track that hovered just along the one thousand feet above sea level contour sweeping before us. As expected of regal demands the pathway was excellent, hard compacted and in sections overlaid with tarmac to ensure that their royal highnesses endure a smooth transition through the estate. It was a very pleasant morning, the skies clear and as we were making good time I took the opportunity to look around me. Balmoral Estate is some 39,000 acres within which lies Lochnagar, arguably the jewel of Deeside. This is the mountain famed by Byron in his poem, Dark Loch na Garr. The mountain, its name actually refers to the loch at the foot of the coire is in fact a series of eleven peaks rather than a single hilltop. In the Gaelic, the original name for Lochnagar was Beinn-nan Ciochan, that is Hill of the Paps in reference to its characteristic peaks.

As we trotted along the track, traversing the foot of Meall Gorm, or Blue Lump, I turned to look to my left then brought Omar to an immediate halt. For a while I sat on a motionless horse, transfixed by the spellbinding sight to the west of me. Like some great towering gothic fortress, the massive mile long coire of Lochnagar stood out black against the beautifully blue, crystal-clear sky. The grand gleaming white snow filled gullies that sub divide the rock faces highlighted the vast sweeping granite buttresses and ridges. For no particular reason, consciously I reached out my gloved hand, almost believing that I could touch this majestic sight immortalised in Byron's words:

> *"England, thy beauties are tame and domestic*
> *To one who has roved o'er the mountains afar:*

Oh for the crags that are wild and majestic!
The steep frowning glories of dark Loch na Garr"

As the Buailteach gates got closer, Fiona Smith in her
Land Rover caught up with me then passed slowly to wait
at the deer fence. For a few moments we chatted then we
set off down the metalled road towards the Royal Lochnagar Distillery Visitor Centre – crew point one. As metalled
hooves clattered on to the public road in the quiet morning
the first hint of fumes discharged from the whisky making
process could be detected in the air but even better was the
waft of coffee that Matt had ready for me.

The Royal Lochnagar Distillery is located just south of
Crathie. Typically, it started life as a small concern; it now
produces one of Scotland's best malt whiskies, allegedly
one of Queen Victoria's favourite drams. John Begg who
was granted a long lease of the site by Abergeldie Estate
started the distillery in 1845. Three years later Queen
Victoria acquired Balmoral, half a mile from the distillery.
In that same year John Begg invited Prince Albert to visit
the distillery. Prince Albert accepted his invitation and
arrived the next day with Queen Victoria and their three
eldest children. Soon thereafter Mr Begg received a Royal
Warrant of Appointment as a supplier to the Queen. The
distillery soon increased in size and the fine Royal Lochnagar, as the brand became known, commanded a high price.
John Begg went on to become a pioneer in the blended
whisky industry, establishing a large trade in blended and
bottled whisky at home and abroad. In 1916, John Dewar
and Sons acquired the distillery but it wasn't until a much
later date that the distillery and machinery, traditionally
powered by water and steam underwent significant alterations to electrical power. Today, despite the widespread use

of automated processes the distillery still retains traditional techniques handed down through generations.

The distillery centre staff were kind and supportive. After a quick replenishment, we set off down the back road towards Crathie and into the grounds of the Balmoral Estate. As the support vehicles overtook me, swung on to the south Deeside road then over the bridge to Crathie, I took the sharp left turn that led uphill past the Post Office. The brief sojourn with cars, tar roads and tourists was quickly over as we headed off along the track through the dense forest. On each side of the pathway although hidden from my view stood the various Cairns erected on the hill tops by Queen Victoria. To the south was the largest of these, erected by Victoria in memory of her beloved husband, Prince Albert; to the north are Princess Beatrice, Princess Alice and Princess Helena's Cairns.

As we approached the first gate, I reached for my map holder to check the route, then realised it was gone. Looking back down the track I spotted the holder laying some fifty metres behind me. I really needed the map, as after Invergelder the Ballochbuie woods can seem like a massive maze. There was no option. I turned to go back. As I did so a Land Rover appeared behind me. I waved it down, pointing to the map holder on the road. The vehicle stopped and out jumped a confused Fiona Smith, thinking I was heading in the opposite direction. She quickly realised what had happened, retrieved the map holder for me then for the third time that day we parted company. I nudged Omar on towards the first deer fence then reached for the catch at the top of the gate. It opened easily, maybe just too easily. Backing Omar away, I pulled the gate gently open to leave enough space to get through.

For the next five minutes I carried out a less than impressive series of dressage manoeuvres that would have mortified a novice. Try as I might I just could not get the horse near enough to reach the catch to close the gate. Exasperated I jumped off, hauled the gate closed, then using the bars of the gate, quickly re-mounted before setting off into the dense forest at a steady trot. Omar was keen to go but as we clicked up a gear the pain from my blistered back was starting to really hurt. To alleviate this I pulled the bum bag around to my side to lessen the pain then sped up moving ever deeper into the forest.

The woods were quiet, peaceful. It was another day of remarkably good weather conditions with just a hint of rising humidity as we walked, trotted, cantered further into the forest. Apart from being surrounded by tall trees on each side of the track, there was little to see. As Alice's Cairn passed to the right, we moved steadily downhill to Invergelder, where the huddle of traditional built cottages and buildings provided a welcome change of scenery. Just as we swung left, the River Dee lay directly ahead of us and to the right the top of Balmoral Castle came briefly into view then receded into the distance as we headed west along the side of the river.

Balmoral has a long history of occupation, beginning as a home built by Sir William Drummond. The estate was formerly owned by King Robert II who held a hunting seat in the grounds and by 1390 a stone castle was built. After Drummond, the estate was sold to Alexander Gordon, the 3^r Earl of Huntly, in the 15th century. The estate remained in the family's hands until it was sold in 1662 to the Farquharsons of Invery, who sold the estate in 1798 to the 2^n Earl of Fife. After leasing the property in 1848, Prince Albert bought full ownership of the estate in 1853 for a sum of £30,000. The present castle, now valued at somewhere nearer £160 million, was built between 1853–1856, planned by William Smith, City Architect of Aberdeen, under the supervison of Prince Albert to make a new and bigger castle fit for the royal family. In 1856 the building was completed with its recognisable pink, light coloured granite taken from the quarries at nearby Glen Gelder. Balmoral Castle is today best known as a royal residence, the summer retreat of Queen Elizabeth II and Prince Phillip, the Duke of Edinburgh.

For the next five kilometres or so we trotted and cantered along a good track, first past the new stud farm for the Queen's Highland and Halflinger ponies, then deeper into the Ballochbuie forest. At times we closed on the river, on its opposite side running parallel was the main Aberdeen to Braemar road. Just as abruptly we disappeared back into the hillside. As civilisation groaned, the noise and bustle of a steady flow of traffic on the other side of the river seemed deafening. As the traffic noise diminished, the silence within the woods was amplified, broken only by the daydreaming clatter of horses hooves. It is interesting to note that this well defined yet unmade route, lined with deep heather, small plantations or towering mature trees was once a public road.

Before the Ballater Turnpike Road Act of 1855 there was a south as well as a north Deeside road. The south Deeside road was a continuation of the present road that runs via Abergeldie to the East Lodge of Balmoral Castle, crossing the Dee at Crathie. Originally, the road continued for six miles through the grounds of Balmoral Estate and Ballochbuie Forest to the Old Bridge of Invercauld. Under the act of 1855, power was taken to close this portion of the south Deeside road. Within special measures obtained in the same period, the Prince Consort undertook the provison of a contemporary bridge over the Dee to carry the new turnpike above the river just slightly west of the old bridge. By 1859, the new bridge was completed and a Public Notice issued in September of that year to the effect that the south

Deeside road as it was then through Balmoral and Ballochbuie was closed to the public and declared a private road.

We trotted on past Connachat Cottage but in my excitement crossing the bridge over the burn missed the memorial that lies close by. Just before the Garbh-alt-Shiel a red deer stag darted out from the woods. On the other side of the track just across from the cottage, a small herd of red deer grazed, ever watchful for intruders. The clatter of hooves caught their attention and they cautiously moved off before we reached the clearing.

Within sight now was the old white painted pedestrian suspension bridge. As I turned left past the foot path leading to the stairs on the footbridge, the distinctive profile of the Old Bridge of Invercauld built in 1859 came into view. This photogenic bridge, the subject of numerous postcards, paintings and book features disappeared again just as quickly as we carried on into the woods, trotting for the last half mile. Approaching the end of the stage near the old bridge, it was a relief to be out of the dense forest. In places it was claustrophobic, even oppressive As we reached the gate at the deer fence where the crew were waiting, I realised that neither the Land Rover nor trailer were there. Although I was glad to see the boys, alarm bells started to ring when I immediately noted the looks of consternation and worry on normally cheery faces.

Spinning the Ground

"Be bold, take the journey the horse is inviting
you on and enjoy what it has to offer."

Wɪᴛʜ the exception of beating a hasty fighting retreat, there were only two ways out of the Ballochbuie Forest. One was to continue on the track that comes out just west of the new bridge, the alternative to cross the narrow gently humped old stone bridge. That afternoon the endurance gods must have been chuckling because one option was, at that immediate point in time, impossible. The alternative? Well! The alternative justified the looks of dismay and apprehension that I had glimpsed just minutes earlier. Effectively to carry on to the new bridge was impossible simply because the gate that I had to go through to get on to the main road then over into Invercauld was well and truly padlocked.

Suddenly I now realised what Fiona Smith had meant about flapping tarpaulins when we chatted at the Builteach gate. Crossing the Old Bridge of Invercauld was the proper route and passable but the second arch closest to our side of the river was undergoing repair works, the stonework draped with bright green tarpaulins. Normally, unless of course you are prone to a green tarpaulin phobia and I am sure someone somewhere is, this would not normally pose a problem. However if you own and ride a spirited pure bred Arabian horse who errs heavily on the side of being an abject wimp at times, then life takes on a whole new meaning. If there is one thing that my horse might not be too keen on, guaranteed to ensure that he leaps spectacularly high enough into the air to cause mayhem. You have guessed it – flapping tarpaulins! And! Colour doesn't matter one scrap.

Naturally, horses do not see the same as humans. As prey animals their sight is a crucial attribute. Horses see less detail than the human eye, but they have a much broader field of vision and that is much more sensitive to movement than humans. Horses cannot see the ground near their front feet, nor can they see their own knees and chest. Mind you there are many humans who are in the same state of disadvantage. However the major difference is that horses have both binocular and monocular vision. In binocular mode the horse will have both eyes focused. In the latter, the horse can see with each eye separately. When a horse sees movement using monocular vision, he will usually turn his head to see with both eyes – switching to binocular vision to focus on the moving object. Confused? Imagine how the horse feels! When the horse switches from monocular to binocular vision, this causes objects to jump and distort until focused on again. So it is not really the fact that it is a polythene bag or tarpaulin tumbling or blowing in the wind that matters, it is the reality that the switch in vision causes an already shifting, fuzzy shape to become even more distorted. That is why this may cause a horse to unexplainably spook. As far as the identification of colour goes, there is no scientific proof either way to support any argument.

Thankfully there was no wind to stir the tarpaulins into scary green monsters. They seemed to be well anchored so I did not really see an issue. But as Paul pointed out very quickly there was just "one tiny little problem" about crossing the bridge. The renovation works actually comprised of re-pointing the stonework. From river level to just above the parapet of the bridge, a network of scaffolding had been erected. Now the catwalk distance between the scaffold lattices at each parapet was wide enough to get a horse through but the headroom Paul thought might just be a touch too low for Omar. Worse still, the middle section was covered in a lot of loosely secured green canvas. And that was a tiny little problem? My stomach heaved. So I went to have a look. My stomach settled a touch. Then I had another look. Then I convinced myself that it was OK. If the satirical guardians of endurance riders doubted my resolve, they were mistaken. Had I lost faith, it would have been one hell of a canter back to Crathie. We had twenty kilometres left to do that day and I selfishly wanted food, sleep and something to relieve the stabbing, stinging pain at the bottom of my spine. So we tucked up the stirrups, then took the spare lead rope from my bum bag and made a loop over Omar's nose to form a makeshift halter – just in case. Taking the reins gently in my right hand, holding the slack with my left we stepped forward slowly towards the ramp, the scaffolding and the scary green tarpaulin monsters. If the horse were going to react it would probably be now. I concentrated hard!

"Whatever you do, don't even look at him".

"Just walk slowly, look straight ahead and he'll be fine". I convinced myself.

And of course he was.

Confidently, we stepped up the incline on to the bridge then assertively walked in between the scaffold network. There was barely enough room for us to squeeze across, the headroom just sufficient. Paul stood in the centre of the bridge after the scaffolding and together we willed and encouraged Omar past the nasty obstacle and scaffolding monsters.

Thankfully, the diminishing contents of three stomachs remained intact. He may well be a wimp at times, but Omar is one very loyal and extremely trusting horse. I doubt if he even blinked once. As soon as we went through the scaffolding on to the open section of bridge, a mutual sigh of relief was probably heard in Braemar ten kilometers away. We quickly jogged over the main road then along a couple of hundred metres of the tree lined entrance drive to Invercauld Castle. Had the horse's first aid kit been readily to hand, I would probably have used the heart monitor on myself. The Land Rover and trailer as it turned out were parked up at the Keiloch a short distance away. Quite safe!

We set off at a brisk trot towards the main house but this lasted for about 400 metres as the first cattle grid and deer fence demarcating the start of the castle grounds, brought me to a halt. Jumping out of the saddle, and then holding the reins in one hand, forced open a wooden slatted pedestrian access gate that probably had not been used in about fifty years. The hinges creaked as I hauled the wooden gate open, dragging it over the deep weed that covered the path. I led Omar through, closed the gate then using the fence as a mounting block was quickly back in the saddle. We passed through the castle policies then to the rear of the impressive Invercauld House. The building, home to the Farquarsons is a large mid-18th century Baronial residence with additions dating through the eighteen hundreds. It is three storeys in height, with a castellated tower rising to seventy feet. At one time the building was a pink colour, a throwback to the days when ox blood was added to the harling as a binding agent. It has since been returned to its original granite blockwork.

Invercauld House sits within impressive parkland and makes for an interesting journey on horseback, the area mainly planted up with larch, the tree for which Invercauld was famous in the 18th century. The house is set on a broad terrace above the park, below which there are the outlines of a square enclosure, possibly a former garden layout. A very long and attractive drive approaches the house from the East Lodge, past the nursery and the pond. There are many tracks and rides through the woodlands to the north of the house, some of which would have been used as woodland drives. Lady Carr's Drive for example, is planted with an avenue of Purple Beech. The policy woodlands are mainly copses of birch, plantations of larch and Scots pine. There are planted roundels, avenues and individual trees in the parks, extensive tracks of commercial plantations throughout the estate. Some of the Scots Pines are thought to be three-four thousand years old. The Forest of Mar was famous in the past and the woods have been described many times in historical accounts; in one, as "the woods are at the same time grand, gloomy and beautiful". That probably sums up the feeling quite well.

At the junction just beyond the main residence we turned to the left away from Alltdourie, the track taking us closer to the River Dee. As we trotted through the open ground, gradually closing with the woods at the southern section of Gleann an t-Slugain, I glanced up towards Beinn a Bhuird. The North Top was shrouded in dark clouds and for the first time that day I became aware that the weather conditions were slowly deteriorating. The first very long groans of thunder encouraged me to move on a little bit faster. But just as the brisk trot before Invercauld was halted by a cattle grid, I now faced a similar exercise to be repeated for the next six gates, some of which were so close together that there was little point in actually re-mounting. It was far quicker to just jog alongside the horse.

Slowly, but steadily we worked our way along the north side of the River Dee passing cottages of substantial granite block yet long since uninhabited. Now in varying states of decay, windows boarded, it seems a travesty that these impressive properties are left unattended. After crossing the bridge that spans the Slugain Burn we passed Balnagower Cottage beyond which stands an obvious solitary monument. The granite obelisk was erected, to the memory of James Farquharson of Invercauld who died in 1862, "by his tenantry and servants, to whom he was greatly attached." It stands on the north bank of the River Dee, near its confluence with the Slugain Burn. Briefly, I laughed then cynically compared this to the monument to the Duke of Sutherland that sits atop the hill of Ben Bhraggie above Golspie. The "Mannie on the Hill" was in his own inimitable way kind of attached to his tenants and servants as well - sufficiently concerned that they were sent packing to a better life elsewhere. Ah! But such was feudal Scotland.

To my left Braemar Castle came into view, then the village. For a very long time Braemar epitomised rural deprivation, content to bask in the glories of Royal Deeside without applying too much effort. Split by the ownership of two different estates such was the tension at one time that the residents of one estate would not cross over the Clunie Water. Nowadays the village is dotted with new properties, has a trendy bistro but nevertheless behind the façade of modernisation there still lies an undertone of indifference. Nevertheless, it was still a welcome sight, the impressive grey stone Invercauld Hotel standing out above the entrance to the village, marking where the old Deeside road had originally come to an end. The hotel also marks the site at where the Earl of Mar started the 1715 rising; the

Jacobite song beginning "The Standard on the Braes of Mar" commemorates it.

As the village passed by, I thought longingly of a hot bath, a meal and a good nights sleep. Shortly after that we were alongside and immediately across the river from our old house near the falls at Corriemulzie. Soon after and just visible in the distance I recognised the prominent rooftop of Mar Lodge, behind which large storm clouds were gathering. Along the valley, out towards the Linn of Dee a thunderstorm was in process, the black clouds were rolling in. In the distance I could hear the steady clap of thunder. The afternoon was heavy on my shoulder as the atmospheric pressure shifted. Clear of fences, gates and cattle grids it was time to move on a bit quicker. After the excitement at the Old Bridge of Dee, I was by now quite relaxed and even of a mind to sing a bit to pass the time. But I thought that the only bit I knew from Queen's Bohemian Rhapsody might be tempting fate just a little.

"Thunderbolts and lightn........." No forget it!

We rattled on over the open stony path, the distance to finishing for the day diminishing by the minute. Although the ground was flat we were still at over a thousand feet above level, the surroundings bare and bleak. To the left, along the margins of the River Dee, the wetlands created where the river had burst its banks or eroded the land was quite obvious. Just west of the Linn of Quoich, the Punchbowl, I could see the Land Rover creeping along the track towards me. For arguments sake, I may as well point out that Quoich should, in proper Gaelic be "cuach" since there is not a "q" in the Gaelic alphabet. The name has probably stuck for mega-years so I am not about to demand that the entire Ordnance Survey mapping database be changed. Anyway, we met up near Allanmore. In the background the thunderstorm was intensifying, there was no place to linger.

We trotted ahead of the vehicle then over the wooden bridge that spans the Water of Quoich then on to the metalled road that leads to Mar Lodge and eventually the Linn of Dee. I felt pleased with myself in the knowledge that we had ticked off five stages and over seven thousand feet of climbing in just two and a half days; I also knew that we were almost finished for the day. Civilisation beckoned. I groaned.

About three hundred metres past the bridge the first streak of lightning flashed across the darkening skies. A tremendous crash of thunder followed. I pulled Omar in to a makeshift parking space at the side of the road, waited for the vehicle to catch up. For the next ten to fifteen minutes we stood tucked in alongside the Land Rover as the deluge poured down on us. I was wet, absolutely sodden. But almost as soon as the storm arrived it was gone, the lightning now only visible to the east along the Dee valley. We pushed on but the tarred road was slippery after the sudden rainfall, slowing us quite dramatically to a gentle walk on the downhill sections. Eventually we reached the woods then made the slight descent down to the east wing of the lodge. Paul took the vehicle ahead to wait at the paddock arranged by Neal Gregory, one of the National Trust staff. As for horse and rider? Well! We took the opportunity to trot majestically past the very front door of the lodge. It's an impressive building, beautifully restored, quite worthy of a backdrop to a knight on a shining horse. OK, I exaggerate, a bit. What really happened was that we did trot past the door of the building, which is impressive. As requested we took a distinguished stand suitably framed by the lodge and hillside behind us for some photographs. And the photograph that appeared in the newspapers a couple of days later did depict a magnificent looking albeit somewhat wet horse. As for the rider? Well! *That photograph* did supreme justice to the fact that he hadn't slept properly for two days, was wrinkled and weather beaten, unwashed, unshaven, bedraggled and soaked to the skin. And no airbrushing!! Imagine that!

Omar was fed; rugged up and turned out into the field at the front of Mar Lodge. In true princely style, the paddock was probably the size of two Hampden Parks. After cleaning up and sorting out some tack for the next day, Paul, Matt and myself set off for the fleshpots of Braemar and our rooms for the night. Thankfully Paul had made the booking, sensibly collected the keys earlier that afternoon. That way, I didn't draw much attention to myself, as quickly passing through the hallway, dodging the ever-watchful eye of the reception desk, I sort of limped, squelched and slithered into the hotel, fearful of anyone seeing me. I was wet, dishevelled, bleary eyed, probably stinking of horse and sweat. The palms of my hands were stained a perfect dark blue colour from the dye out of my riding gloves. I could just imagine the NO VACANCIES sign going up as I approached. The pain in my back was growing worse forcing me to grimace as I heaved my travel bag up the numerous flights of stairs to our attic quarters. I was not a very appealing sight.

The room was cosy, ample for an overnight stay. In fact, in comparison to the last two nights, it was luxury. Before I set about unpacking my immediate necessities, finding somewhere to start drying out my clothes, I decided to pay the local store a visit in the hope that I might find some antiseptic cream for my back. Although not able to see what damage existed I reasoned that whatever it was, the skin needed some attention, the idea of plundering the horses first aid kit for herbal gel an unlikely option. So I descended the myriad flights of stairs then dodging the reception desk, sort of limped, squelched and slithered out of the hotel. The village was quite busy. Hill walkers and cyclists adorned the tables and chairs outside the Fife Arms, sipping pints of beer in the afternoon warmth. The thunderstorm and rain had long since passed to leave the typically fresh clean air in its aftermath. Since most of these people had obviously spent a hard day on the hill, their clothing suitably scarred by the experience, I actually believed that I blended in. My self-consciousness disappeared almost to the point that I nearly scoffed when one hill bashing Lycra clad cyclist was overheard, in a voice designed for all to hear, his harsh ride over some minor hill and forest tracks.

The one and only mini-supermarket in the village was easily found. There wasn't really a great deal of choice in the narrow aisles. Search as I might, I could not find the sort of antiseptic cream that I needed. Finally my eyes came to rest upon the basic stock of baby goods and there beheld a solitary tub of nappy rash cream. For some obscure reason, I thought that the shortage might have been due to a recent run on cream for saddle sores or alternatively the three hundred plus population of Braemar were undergoing a sudden, no doubt unexpected baby boom. Given the average age of the population, the thought made me shiver. Discounting the latter, then stifling a loud guffaw I imme- diately thought of the loud-mouthed cyclist outside the pub. Poetic justice, I hoped! I speedily scanned the label and to my relief decided that this might just do the trick. Hastening to the counter I quickly paid for the jar of cream without a hint of embarrassment then with head held high marched as best and as rapidly as I could back to the hotel.

In my room wet clothes were stripped off. My riding boots and socks were saturated, jodhpurs and riding jacket wet through. I hung these over the radiator to dry then set about examining the nether regions of my posterior. It wasn't a pretty sight but first of all I had to peel off my boxer shorts, firmly stuck to the raw skin. That brought the first tears to my eyes. I turned my uncovered rear end to look in the mirror exposing the full extent of the mess that passed for my lower back. From the base of my spine then down over my buttocks, the skin had been completely worn away to leave a bright red blister the size of a human's palm. Obviously the blister had burst long since; the fluid loss had fused into my boxers then acted as an effective adhesive. What had caused the burn were the airflow pads on my heavily laden bum bag chafing against my lower spine.

After shaving, I ran a deep bath, adjusting the temperature to make the anticipated painful task somewhat easier. Tentatively I stepped into the bath, the warm water felt fine. I grasped each side of the bath then slowly sheepishly lowered myself downwards. As the warm water reached the first part of the wound, I leapt back up with a yelp, smacking my head on the shower curtain rail. A touch more cold water went into the bath. Slowly, I sank down again. This time I locked my teeth together, clenched my jaw. As the water enfolded the friction burn, I cursed aloud as the sharp, stinging, stabbing pain shot through me. The stinging seemed to last for ever. Then it passed. For the next twenty minutes I basked in the warm water, occasionally topping up the heat. I could feel my muscles relax, the tiredness draining away. I dried myself off very carefully then applied a liberal slab of nappy rash cream. The soothing effect was immediate.

Now cleaned up, washed and in fresh clothing, amongst the plethora of tourists I even felt human. Taking the opportunity to phone Rose, the first time in three days, she was enthusiastically briefed on the status of my backside. She was however less than impressed! I missed her and looked forward to seeing her the next day at Blair Atholl. Eventually, we joined the throng of bus parties in the large dining room. For the first time in days I sat down to a proper meal, relishing the comfort and service. It may not have been the best meal in the world but I ate everything in front of me, bread rolls and soup, haggis, neeps and tatties, vegetables then cheese and biscuits. Foodies and health freaks may scoff but I enjoyed it immensely. Its all very well living on a diet of high-energy athletic foods, muscle recovery and electrolyte drinks as I had been for a couple of days but my meal that night was food for the gods. I couldn't wait for breakfast. We chatted over the meal, discussed the plans for next day, then as our plates were finally cleared away; we were approached by one of the hotel staff.

"Tea and coffee is served in the lounge gentlemen," advised the Restaurant Manager.

So we left our table and went in search of the lounge. Racked against the wall on a white linen clothed table sat the tea, coffee, cups and saucers. But there was not one seat to be had. The place was packed solid with the overtly cheery contents of two "blue rinse" coach tour parties. At the end of the room sitting close to the window was the obligatory folk musician, strumming freely on a traditional guitar. Now, at the best of times I could never be described as a sociable, gregarious person. The thought of being trapped in this room while a jolly teeth flashing folk singer rattled out Bebbington Bush, expecting the audience to join in the chorus was too much for me. Experience had taught me that even worse was the idea that I might be singled out, targeted for not singing and that almost sent me into a full-blown panic attack. I looked at Paul. Paul looked at me. Matt looked horrified. So just after nine o'clock we took the decision to forego the coffee and associated entertainment, climbed the myriad of stairs and went to bed. Symbolically at least, I had now transcended from a hell-raising past into the realms of an existence where a nourishing meal, good nights sleep and a jar of nappy rash cream epitomised ecstasy.

That night I slept like the proverbial log but woke early as the first light of dawn shone through the curtains. I peeked out of the window, dismayed to see that the village was encased in very low cloud, thick drizzle forming a dense blanket. I had hoped for a better forecast. After washing, the blob of cream was dully applied. The burn was still painful but it had eased. Swapping the still sodden black jodhpurs for a light beige pair I dressed in my riding clothes, but I put a pair of trousers on over the jodhpurs. I had no intention of prancing around in tight riding gear over breakfast in front of fifty elderly women. That might just be a bit too much for them. I had no desire to be irresponsible!

As it was too early for breakfast I walked into the village. The drizzle was heavy, the cloud base not much higher than the church tops but to the west, I optimistically concluded that the clouds were breaking. Perhaps the forecast would be right after all. Nothing seemed to have changed much. The pub at the back of the hotel where we had supped our pints years ago after a days stalking was in a near derelict state. There were new properties, bistro with the mandatory exorbitant prices and a shop selling climbing gear. But otherwise Braemar had changed very little although it is still an interesting district. The ancient castle of Kindrochit or bridge end, which gave Braemar its original name of Castleton, *Baile Chaisteil*, stood close to the bridge over the Clunie but only its foundations remains. Feeling a tad hungry after the morning stroll, I walked back over the Clunie Bridge to the hotel to meet Paul and Matt. We then joined the queue of ravenous tourists waiting outside the restaurant for breakfast.

As we drove back to Mar Lodge, we could see that the clouds were breaking up quite rapidly, promising another fine settled day. Far out to the west, the skies were clearing. Approaching the lodge, we spotted Omar, typically at the furthest end of the paddock being feted over the fence by some adults and children. As I led him back to the gate and trailer for his breakfast, I could see that he was alert, eager, suffering no ill effects. As he munched his morning meal, we tidied up the trailer, sorted out the tack, finalised the plan for the day. Paul and Matt were faced with a long haul from Braemar over Cairnwell to pick up the A9 near Pitlochry then on to Blair Atholl where David Greer, Head of Rural Development at Atholl Estates had arranged a paddock for Omar close to the castle. We were also given permission to take the Land Rover from the village as far up the private road to Forest Lodge and Glen Tilt as necessary, thereby giving us more flexible support.

For me, in terms of navigation, it was a straightforward ride through a glen that has witnessed a wide range of history. At the end of 1771, the noted naturalist and anti-quary Thomas Pennant published *A Tour in Scotland in 1769*, which proved remarkably popular and was followed in 1774 by an account of another journey in Scotland, in two volumes. These works have proved invaluable in preserving a record of important antiquarian relics which have now perished. Pennant however described his journey through Glen Tilt as " the most dangerous and most horrible I have ever travelled." And on that happy thought – off we went.

It was mid morning, but already cars full of walkers and mountain cyclists were streaming over the bridge at the start of the track near the Linn of Dee. Of course the Arabian couldn't resist responding to the admiring looks aimed in his direction. Quite possibly the young ladies were admiring me? OK! - Just a thought! In retrospect it probably was Omar.

"C'mon Omar no-one is looking at You!"

Snort!

"Man, you really are a poseur. Lets trot on for a while."

Snort!

Really! It must be an Arabian horse thing. Too intent on looking around, proud heads held high, tails in towering banners, to see if anyone might just be watching them, admiring that incomparable attractive regal-ness, the next thing is that they will trip over their own feet – hooves! Honestly!

We trot on. It's another day, another distance to achieve. Once again my world became framed by the narrow space just ahead and in front of a pair of tipped in ears - nothing else mattered. Muscles to warm up – concentrate, focus. We quickly caught up with the party of walkers who were heading for the Larig Ghru, then just as quickly they receded into the distance along with the tree line that marked the cleft in the valley at the Linn of Dee.

At the Chest of Dee, the confluence where the Alt-an-t-Sleilich meets the River Dee we clattered over the good solid White Bridge. To the north the track bent away towards the Larig Ghru, *Gruesome Pass*, the Pools of Dee and the heartland of the Cairngorms, the high tops of Cairn Toul, Braeriach and Ben Macdhui. These are all mountains over four thousand feet and still held a vast quantity of snow. We trotted on sedately along the edge of the woods past the old ruin of Ruigh nan Clach, a place where probably cattle once came for summer grazing. No doubt cattle drovers also used the shieling as they worked their way south to Blair Atholl then onwards to the famous Falkirk Tryst. With each steady footfall we got deeper into the narrowing glen. It is spectacular countryside, wild landscape of craggy tops, steep heather clad hillsides. The early morning mist had cleared, leaving brighter more settled skies, an idyllic day.

At any other time it would have been a place to linger. But for us we had a task. A few minutes later we reached the ford where the Geldie Burn meets the Alt-an-t-Sleilich. The approach to the ford looked fine, a nice easy gradient slanting down into the river then out again at the opposite side. What didn't look like an immediate source of fun was the height and velocity of the river? The heat of the past few days had created a fairly substantial snowmelt. Combined with the thunderstorm of the previous afternoon, this of course had put the rivers and wide burns, all tributaries of the Dee into spate.

Omar was gently nudged towards the river. He easily stepped down the gradient then hesitated. I backed him off, turned then nudged him on again. He was not keen. In fact he was downright rebellious. I tried again. He stepped forward as far as the water's edge then stopped – abruptly. Now there were two things I could do. One being to drive him on into the water but that risked a slip even an injury for both of us. It is one thing being turfed off into snow but the prospect of a mid morning bath in the tumbling icy waters of the Geldie Burn was a different proposition. Being the better part of discretion, I took the cowards option and got off. The water was deep, fast flowing, typically stained dark brown from the peat run off. Even as I got closer to the edge I still couldn't see the bottom but could just make out some very large rounded stones, the tops of which were scarcely covered. I took a deep breath then waded into the water, my boots skidding on the stones. It was cold, enough to catch my breath. As I searched frantically for the shortest way across and away from the larger boulders, first the water came over my boots, then up to my shins, then my knees. As the water surged around my lower thighs I ploughed on, Omar obediently following me. Very quickly I felt the stones crunch securely under my boots. At the far bank, I accelerated; together we jumped up over the soft bank then instantly were back on solid ground.

If a record exists for a time taken between the burn and the ruins of Bynack Lodge, we probably hold it. Crossing the next two fords was easier but they were much more shallow, without hesitation Omar just waded through at the first attempt. At the ruined lodge I stopped just long enough to pull off my boots, drain out the water and wring out my socks. The jodhpurs would dry out eventually with the heat from my legs. Omar fussed around looking for some tasty grass morsel then as the water poured from my footwear he gave out one of his typical disapproving Arabian snorts.

At one point I remembered as a young teenager, the lodge with its rooms and roof intact. Today it stands forlorn and derelict, torn apart for firewood by inconsiderate, unthinking hill walkers whose priorities seem to lie far away from the wilderness they allegedly aspire to enjoy. We left the old lodge behind us. Just beyond that we followed the track briefly back towards the river then took an immediate sharp right. From there the trail that starts off just feet from the banks of the Alt-an-t-Sleilich, deteriorates quite suddenly. The transition from a good solid Land Rover track to a narrow, muddy rock lined footpath became very apparent when Omar took sight of the dark shining peat hag that lay directly in front. For the second time that morning he rebelled. All we had to do was jump across the slight ditch but that was easier said than done. This time I bribed him with a Polo mint. Seconds later we were clattering along the narrow path heading into Pennant's bleak, melancholy horrible tract of landscape.

From Bynack the path climbs gently, keeping fairly high to avoid the bog and marshland that lies in the floor of the valley. Queen Victoria travelled through here in 1861, her two pipers striking up "The Athole Highlanders" as she approached Bynack or according to Robert Smith, *Bainoch*, as she pronounced it. Apparently, the Queen regarded the journey as "rather a hazardous proceeding, at least an adventurous one, and what the road was." If anything the stretch between Bynack and the Falls of Tarf has changed little at all. To call this a road is really a bit more than an optimistic over-exaggeration. Travelling on it in good daytime conditions is still something of an adventure. In the immediate distance the glen was wide, the hillsides smooth and rounded dropping to the river but that was soon to change as we worked our way deeper into the claustrophobic vertigo inducing, constricted gorge of Glen Tilt.

The path was narrow but easy to follow. About a kilometre or so from Bynack we started to climb the first rise that leads slowly uphill to the uppermost section of the road. Very soon we were picking and weaving our way along a track that alternated between a hard rock surface and wet peat covered earth. It was slow progress. Omar had to be carefully manoeuvred past sections of track where boulders encroached on the sides or over steps of earth where the original path had been washed away. There was little time to look around. Instead my concentration remained firmly fixed in negotiating the hillside as we contoured our way around the lower stretches of Cnapan nan Clach. To the south the steep side of Meall Tionail with the rising slopes of the Sron a Bhoididh dominated the view. It was here with the waters of Dubh alt an Beag crashing down into the valley floor that the evident steepness of the opposite hillside became very real. What also started to become very real was the sudden drop in the hillside between the narrow path, the valley floor and me.

Glen Tilt effectively begins in the confines of Aberdeenshire then runs in a southwesterly direction, concluding at Blair Atholl. If a wilderness area can be defined by proximity to, or remoteness from a public road, then this area would undoubtedly qualify. This is the site of one of the main geological faults in the region. From the northwest the glen appears wide almost open moorland, the hills rounded and green. These are covered in grassy vegetation including much moss and heath. As the lower slopes tend to be gradual, thick layers of peat have built up. There is a feeling of space although far from being featureless.

But once the imaginary line that runs down the sharp apex of the Sron a Bhoididh is crossed, the valley takes on a different veneer. From here the glen becomes narrower, rockier. The impression of wide-open spaces gives way to confined ruggedness, claustrophobic constriction. For this is the notorious Garrabuie or *garbh buidhe* ravine once described "as like a gigantic canal cutting." Perhaps, owing to its narrowness and difficulty in negotiating the glen, this was never a popular route for the cattle drovers. I could now understand why as this is allegedly one of the deepest ravines in the British Isles.

Throughout history, travellers from across a wide spectrum of commercial necessity or leisurely choice have used the thoroughfare. The "road" was also the subject of a Court of Session decree. In the 1840s the Duke of Atholl tried to close the glen. The Scottish Rights of Way Society who won the historic landmark case challenged this action. The Ballad of Glen Tilt tells the story of how Professor J Hutton Balfour with a party of botanists went there. An angry Duke challenged them but with an impertinent closure, the poem substantiates the outcome.

"There ne'er a kilted chiel
Shall drive us back this day, man.
Its justice and its public richt,
Well pass Glen Tilt afore the nicht."

In military circles today Glen Tilt is known as Star Wars Alley. It is also one of the few remote Scottish areas in Google Earth that is shown in high resolution. For it is through here in the narrow confines of the Garrabuie and Ruigh an Fhirich in perfect terrain that the RAF practice their low-level fighter runs. With full justification, I didn't really relish the idea of being buzzed by the afterburners of a Tornado jet whilst negotiating a spirited horse along these dangerously narrow sections. So just in case, I had been advised to contact air traffic control at RAF Leuchars. I was met with a very kind and polite response to the query that as I would be riding through there and could they tell me if there were any fast jets scheduled for that day. The WRAF on duty advised that I had nothing to worry about - no flights took place on a Sunday. I should have known from my own days in the MoD, and I hope that I am not infringing any aspects of the Official Secrets Act that Sunday is not a day for conflict!! Nevertheless, I was relieved.

Sitting atop a small hill just east of Loch Tilt there stands a cairn. As we passed below this we crossed back over the imaginary line marking the Cairngorms National Park and into Perthshire. The highest point of the route was over. From then on in it was all a gradual though not specifically easy descent. As we slowly deliberately worked our way along the path towards the Falls of Tarf, the going deteriorated. The trail perched precariously on the steep sloping hillside became narrower, rockier in places. Caution was needed; a slip here would have been catastrophe. In places, we dropped down to the edge of the river, then just as suddenly the track veered back up onto the steep hill. For two miles we negotiated this claustrophobic, vertigo inducing section of path that seemed to be endless. This was no place to loose one's nerve, nowhere to stop and rest, so we pressed on. Walking now, I led Omar over the rock steps, through the overabundance of twinkling burns, across bog and wet peat. In a sense this was a supreme adventure playground for rider and horse, an ultimate test of faith but not for the faint hearted. Not far ahead where the Tarf Water plunges through a deep rocky gorge to join the Tilt another unplanned sense of adventure waited!

As we approached the Falls of Tarf, I spotted mountain bikers ahead of me, pushing their cycles over a difficult section. I also saw the confines of the hillside and a further rocky section so I decided to wait for them to pass. They had the same idea. Typically we met in the middle where the track runs close to the river. For a few minutes we chatted. They had a long laborious run ahead of them to the Linn of Dee. I didn't envy them the trip. Ahead of me, there was one difficult rocky section to bypass before the falls. I quickly surveyed the obstacle then stepped down towards the burn, close to where the path to Fealar crosses, gently manoeuvred Omar up the steep rock on the other side then marched on. Before I turned the corner towards the falls, I glanced back. The cyclists, a couple from Edinburgh were watching, obviously relieved to see us back on reasonably easy solid ground.

Thankfully, the Bedford Bridge, erected in 1886 by the Scottish Rights of Way Society had been recently modernised and strengthened by the British Army. The alternative was the ford at the confluence of the waters just below. The bridge over the tumbling water thirty feet below seemed the better option. Not hesitating I marched Omar straight up the ramp then on to the wooden bridge. Within a couple of steps the structure started to sway gently, just enough to induce a stomach churning sensation. My legs wobbled as I fought to balance myself. As the bridge started to oscillate, I did not dare to look down. I swear at that point Omar, like some Loony Tunes cartoon character, went onto his tiptoes. Tempted through urgency and a growing sense of panic to hasten the steps, we took it steadily. From stepping on to the ramp at one end to getting back on to the path on the other side probably took about thirty seconds. It just seemed interminable.

At the foot of Creag an Dubh, the path swings onto an almost perfect south-westerly direction; where the entire extent of the remaining section of glen becomes clearly evident. As we climbed a further rise, the first of the plantations north east of Forest Lodge came into view. Ahead of me I could see the widening glen, the hills again more smooth and rounded as we gradually descended towards the more fertile plain of the River Garry and Perthshire. Colours were changing. The subdued brown and bleached hues of the open moor and hillside gave way to a multitude of greenery. Near Dun Beag we passed the Old Shielings then joined the main estate track that sweeps its way down to Blair Atholl. It was a pleasure to be back on firm ground. As we climbed one more rise, I glimpsed the Land Rover inching its way along the private road then pull into the grass at the side of the river. Within minutes we were reunited.

"Hi Omar. How are you?" enquired my wife as she reached to hold the reins. Then to me as an afterthought,

"Why haven't you been wearing your sunglasses? Your eyes are all puffy."

I just smiled, finished my obligatory cool drink, dumped the bum bag then prepared to set off for the final leg of the day's distance. Apparently close to where we stopped there is a stone with a "13" carved into it. This denotes the distance in miles from that point to Blair Atholl. The stone must have been close but I certainly didn't see it.

After the brief rest, we trotted off along the last section of road for the paddock near to Blair Castle. Forest Lodge then Marble Lodge passed, the latter probably owing it name to the fact that marble was once quarried in the glen. We hammered along the estate road, only slowing for the occasional cattle grid or anxious sheep. According to Pennant during his adventure through Glen Tilt, this part of the road was so badly rutted that horses often had to cross their legs to find a secure spot for their feet. Steadily the miles diminished. We raced the Land Rover along the track, riding downhill, spinning the ground! Gradually the open wilderness of the glen receded. We switched places with the vehicle to let them get ahead, to clear the way through the cattle grids, and then we picked up speed again. Soon we were high above the ravine with the River Tilt tumbling below us, the sound of its waters penetrated the still afternoon. We passed into a mixture of trees, native and planted conifers, groves of alders, gnarled ancient birch. The road dropped down. We clattered over the Old Bridge of Tilt, the sound of steel shod hooves shattering the afternoon silence then we swung right towards the Castle policies. As we chased the Land Rover along the sheltered, tree-lined track towards Blair Atholl something on my left caught my eye. A white and brown shape keeping pace with us darted in and out of the undergrowth. My concentration was firmly fixed on keeping up the speed, getting finished for the day, the expectation of some decent food and a good nights rest. But I was puzzled.

The Ghost of Rannoch

"Only those who dare to fail greatly, can ever achieve greatly"

THE ride through Glen Tilt had been a significant milestone. Pennants "horrible" glen was behind us. The journey through the Cairngorms was over. With it we had covered well in excess of over half the distance from coast to coast, climbed and descended over 9000 feet of remote, rugged terrain. The sudden contrast from the open moor, the confines of the glen; the steepness of the craggy hillsides to the almost flat arable nature of the Perthshire countryside and the Garry valley around Blair Castle was abrupt. The quiet solitude of Glen Tilt deceased quite dramatically as we trotted the last couple of kilometres into the policies of the imposing, impressive Blair Castle. Suddenly, or so it seemed, it was back to the hustle and bustle of everyday life. Cars moved around, the shouts and cries from the nearby caravan park seemed to amplify the fact that crowds of holidaymakers, tourists, or just simply those on some mundane travelling excursion now surrounded us. In the distance, the movement of traffic along the infamous A9 could just be heard. The clatter of the train passing through the nearby railway station in Blair Atholl on the Inverness to Glasgow rail line seemed surreal. Life seemed to have changed pace once again. The isolation of the preceding hills and glens seemed a long way off when all too soon we were at the paddock. But there was no time for idealistic contemplation. Another stage was finished; the end of day routine took over.

Omar was fed, watered, pampered by a throng of his fan club then turned out to his temporary paddock at Blair Castle. Paul, Matt, Rose, and the rest of the gang piled into their vehicle then headed off home. During the periods of remoteness with just Omar for company, I had never actually felt cut off but now I felt a sudden twinge of loneliness as I watched them go, especially sorry to say goodbye to Paul and Matt. Their support and assistance over the last few days had been invaluable, their contribution made the success of completing six fast stages possible. It was a pleasure to see father and son not only working together but also enjoying each other's company and the experience. Each phase had been accomplished with their help, well disciplined routines made easy. My job was to ride and they let me get on with it whereas they did the daily planning, liaison with numerous contacts, the advance preparation. On arrival at each stage or crewing point, everything was ready. As the days had passed their fondness for Omar became more apparent, in turn the horse became more comfortable in their presence. But it was time to carry on with the plan; the arrangements had been made to change the support crew. Accordingly I knew this was coming. So I set off into the village to meet Marc Millson who would be taking over for the rest of the ride.

It was still early evening, pleasantly warm. Blair Atholl bustled with people, tourists mostly; easily identifiable by the relaxed casual garb of baggy shorts and floppy tee shirts. We checked into a local hotel then before our evening meal went back to the paddock to ensure that Omar was settled for the night. He was liberally sprayed with insect repellent, adorned with a fly mask then turned back out to the immense field. Satisfied that he was comfortable with sufficient hay and water and a huge paddock to keep him amused, we returned to the hotel to relax over the meal. The planning for the following day was pretty straight forward as the main aim was to reach Rannoch Station by early afternoon. The accommodation for humans at the end of the next stage had all been arranged, Omar's paddock prepared. The only arduous part of the day ahead was the mid numbing sections of road that were necessary to get there. There were no alternatives because in effect the River Garry, the A9 trunk road and the Inverness railway line boxed us in. The original plan was to cross over to Inverack then cut through the edge of the forests down into Tressait on the edge of Loch Tummel. But with the bridge at Baluain down, there was no direct access across the river then over the A9. Any immediate thoughts about moving along one of the most notorious trunk roads in Scotland didn't even bear thinking about. So with that in mind, there was only one way to go and that was by the tarmac side roads that start under the A9 near the House of Bruar then skirt the north side of Glen Errochty.

If I thought that I would be able to sleep well that night, I was again mistaken. The pain in my back had eased as the antiseptic cream took effect but it still hurt. It had been a long day, tiring, somewhat physically draining but enough I thought to ensure that I would drift off quite easily. I was wrong. Midnight came and went. I tossed and turned as my mind raced over the last twenty-four hours, then sought out the next. There was nothing to worry about or occupy my mind with concern. On the contrary everything to date had gone extremely well. If anything I basked in the flushes of success, my mind racing backwards and forwards over the terrain that had been crossed. I mentally searched out problems then solutions, and then lessons learnt. I switched on the television, made a cup of tea but nothing could alleviate the adrenalin that continued to rush through me. For a while I tried to read. Eventually around two o'clock I must have finally managed to drop off. Typically, the next thing I knew, daylight was bursting through the window, the alarm sounding its morning call. Time to be on the move again. After a decent breakfast we caught up Omar who was hiding close to the bushes on the north side of the paddock, fly mask discarded somewhere out of sight where he had shed the embarrassing frilly garment during the night. His call for breakfast needed no second telling though.

From Blair Atholl the route took a westerly direction past Old Blair, through Calvine then on under the A9 to Trina-four. The bustle of traffic from the A9 receded as the road cut into the hillside before descending to Kinloch Rannoch. From here we had originally planned to follow the north edge of the loch to Bridge of Gaur but instead opted for the quieter albeit narrower minor road that runs along the south side past the Tay Forest Park. We lingered for a while at the shore of Loch Rannoch, its entire twelve-mile length stretched out in sparkling clear waters. In the far distance the hills of Glencoe could just be seen, behind us Schiehal-lion reared its sugarloaf bulk. For yet another day, the weather remained on our side, the heat shimmering on the mountains around us, the skies almost cloudless. It would have been easy to hang around, to admire our beautiful countryside, and bask in the surroundings. As Albert Einstein said:

> *"Look deep into nature, and then you will understand everything better."*

But the plan didn't allow us to linger; all we knew by now was to keep moving, maintain the momentum.

Nothing else mattered. Muscles ached – ride. Muscles warmed up – ride faster. Rest was a brief stop in the saddle or to slosh down Omar. Food was high energy liquid from a plastic bottle. All that I saw in front of me, or immediately cared about was framed just beyond my horse's alert listening tipped in ears. Omar marched on as usual, ever alert, ever vigilant and occasionally looking around him to see if anyone might just be looking at him, admiring his proud desert and regal "handsomeness". What was behind me now was distance because that was exactly where I wanted it. Done! Over! For the time being, there was no interest in what was behind us or what had been achieved. The routine was a simple case of just keep pushing on - always seeking out the next opportunity for a further burst of speed. Sleep by now was a luxury. Fatigue became narcotic. As a rough guide, a horse makes one hundred different muscle movements in ten minutes. Each one of those is transmitted to the rider. Ten minutes equals one hundred muscle movements; one hour equals six hundred muscle movements and so on. Think the physics of metals and the limits of endurance - the point where stress and fatigue cause failure.

But this was not based on the algorithms of mathematics or physics. It was a world of unremitting heat, dehydration, concentration, constant movement, muscular activity minute by minute, hour after hour. Now it was into day after day. There was neither respite nor any sought. The steady clip clop of feet hitting hard surfaces, the zing of steel shoes on tarmac or stones seemed to induce a hypnotic trancelike state with an all-consuming sense of sheer pleasure, endless euphoria. The months of gruelling training and preparation, the intense often-unforgiving nature of the required conditioning were paying dividends.

To the innocent bystander it may well have seemed that we functioned in a mindless, disinterested state, locked in a mental condition of unthinking neutrality. But they would have been completely wrong because automaticity is the ability to do things without occupying the mind with the low level details required, the ability to disengage the brain from the surrounding trivia. What in actual fact was happening was the single-minded immersion of energised focus, full involvement and success in the process of the activity. According to the psychoanalyst Mihaly Csikszent-mihaly this is the perfect state of performance, focused motivation - being in the "flow". This state of mind is perhaps the ultimate in harnessing the emotions in the service of performing. In flow the sensations are not just contained and channelled but positive, energised and aligned with the task in hand. To be caught in the ennui of depression or the agitation of anxiety is to be barred from the flow. The real hallmark of flow is a feeling of spontane-ous joy, even rapture while performing a task. Colloquial terms for this or similar mental states are "on the ball, in the groove or in the zone". The plan may well have been in charge but we marched on, happy willing players in a game that was now pushing the extremes of endurance – and by simple definition, nothing more than the ability to with-stand prolonged strain, extended athletic output over a comprehensive distance or for an extended period of time.

By mid morning the weather stayed kind. The days of continuous warm, almost tropical weather seemed remark-ably unreal. Even although we were now pushing deeper towards the west coast and its notorious reputation for lengthy periods of precipitation, ambient conditions remained dry and warm. The thought of plodding through continual rain and slippery conditions, or soaked to the skin for days made me shiver. May had been chosen as the month most likely to provide the best, driest conditions, statistically offering the best chance of success. The choice was good, even better than expected, the temperatures higher than calculated. Thankfully, the weather did not offer any delays or problems. Despite the continual concerns or apprehension in moving along narrow twisting roads this part of the route was easy, bounded on one side by Loch Rannoch, the Tay Forest Park on the other. The miles clicked by. At the Bridge of Gaur, we called in to see Nick and Christine Thetford. Nick is Head Gamekeeper for Lord Pearson of Rannoch Barracks Estate. Nick's wife Christine had organised the accommodation for humans and horse at Rannoch Station and helped enormously with the preparations for crossing the moor. We joined them and Iain the fishing ghillie for lunch and discussions for the following day. It was very easy to delay leaving, as all three are affable company. But having scoffed enough of Christine's homemade bread, cheese and ham sandwiches, we probably outstayed our welcome. Anyway Omar stood waiting patiently. It was time to bid a polite farewell.

From the farm at Invercomrie, the road led out over the narrow old stone bridge that spans the Gaur as it flows past the big house itself. The property owes it name to its construction in the 1700s as a base for the Government forces that came to patrol the highlands and maintain some form of legislative control. Once over the bridge, we turned left on to the B846 finally starting to collect some direct westerly direction.

The road from Bridge of Gaur to Rannoch Station is not exactly pleasant. Despite the fact that the road stops abruptly at the railway line, it remains a popular outing for tourists. Perhaps that is what makes it popular – a drive along a road that goes nowhere apart from the sight of a picturesque building set amid some spectacular scenery.

In effect it is a narrow road but not officially classed as a single-track route. It should be. But it's a gentle undulating road through a mixture of scenery and terrain that belies the short distance of six miles. For the first couple of miles the road bounded by forest, *Coille Bhienie,* on the north side, twists and winds its way close to the edge of the boulder laced River Gaur. Gradually it climbs up through a section of farmland at Dunan before reaching the hydroelectric power station at the head of Loch Eigheach. From then on in the road shifts its twisting snakelike progress out on to the edge of open hillside before turning due west at the head of the loch.

Thankfully, the traffic was light. With the Land Rover and trailer tucked in a few hundred metres at the back, I felt safe in the knowledge that nothing could sneak up directly behind me, leaving me to focus on the road ahead. As we started the gentle trot up along the short incline from the power station, we met the first group of walkers taking part in The Great Outdoor Challenge. They looked exhausted. Obviously the heat was taking its toil. Diplomatically, I kept my mouth shut. From the head of Loch Eigheach the road cuts through open moor then finally, as if intent on a definitive last sprint, makes a straight dash across the edge of open moor to come to rest at the picturesque railway station that effectively sits in the middle of nowhere but adorns the bleak inhospitable landscape around it. At the south end of the railway station near to the level crossing, a Scottish Rights of Way Society green painted sign points the way for the footpath:

TO GLENCOE
12 MILES

And that belied just a bit more than a certain degree of harsh reality.

As we crossed the railway line just south of the station, to follow the track to Iain's cottage at Cruach, the vast sweep of the moorland to the south just beyond Dubh Lochan became a sudden sharp reminder of certainty. On my right the steep sides of dense forest blocked a line of sight to the north and west but I knew what was there or thought I knew what to expect.

Even on a nice pleasant summer's day, Rannoch Moor is a bleak desolate piece of landscape. In its entirety the moor covers approximately ninety square miles of land that is little more than wet peat hag interspersed with a plethora of streams, small inky black lochans and great sweeps of lochs. It is a natural drainage system where the peat layer is some thirty feet deep in places. The information plaque at the Rannoch Railway Station is right and pulls no punches. *This is not an area to trifle with.* It is worthwhile advice. Legend may well abound with tales of witches, ghosts and the supernatural but the harsh reality of man's ventures onto this bleak moor bear a more grim sense of danger than any ghostly tale. The character changes not only with the seasons but almost daily dependant on the prevailing weather conditions. A day in August can produce dry firm walking conditions. Twenty-four hours later after a spell of rain, the wet, dangerous boggy conditions become all too obvious.

From the bleak greys and browns of the matt grasses and decayed heather so evident in April and May, the moor bursts into life with an impressive array of purple shades of heather. The moor becomes a wilderness of green but alive with a magnitude of colour from a vast array of plant life from bog asphodel to fluffy waving cotton grass. Within this deceptive setting it was here that the original reconnaissance party for the railway almost perished to a man in a storm. Had this happened, the lifeline of a railway that links the central belt with the western highlands would probably never have been constructed? Equally so, as one Robert McAlpine was a member of the surveying party, it is also highly likely that the famous civil engineering dynasty that exists today wouldn't have been created. But they survived and the railway line running north – south across the moor, floated on birch scrub, earth and potash, cut deep into the massive peat layer, endures to this day.

On a previous occasion I walked from Rannoch Station out on to the moor with Rose and Tig. It was a pleasant enough stroll through the pine scented forest track before we reached the open hillside that soon gave way to the evident bleakness of the moor itself. In the distance the massive bulk of the Buachaille Etive Mor, "*Big Shepherd of Etive*", towered beyond Kingshouse and the adjacent A82. Almost within touching distance were the small forest plantations close to the Black Corries Lodge where the hard track continued past the telecomms mast and extended out onto the moor. We traced the path through the gates at the deer fence then high above the edge of Loch Laidon to the rusted corrugated iron roof of the old cottage Tigh na Cruaiche, "*the house of rubble*". From there the track bends away from the line of electric poles to higher ground and as it does so, becomes narrower but firmer. But I was uncomfortable. We walked on slowly, deeper into the moor following a barely discernible track that led out into the bleakness of this alien landscape. The further we walked, the more wet and boggy the terrain became. Even sticking with the path proved to be difficult. Rose stayed behind as I continued on past the deer fence. With each step I sank just that little bit deeper, boots squelching under the soft peat laden surface. But this was very early spring, there was hard ground ahead of me and this was encouraging. Convinced that a good dry spell would surely improve the conditions, I carried on with the plan to cross an area that for all accounts hadn't been ridden over in the last 100 years.

Now sometime later we threw our bags into the sparse, basic rooms and settled into Renton Cottage just across the other side of the railway line where the bust of its namesake glares eternally southwards over the moor. Neither fazed nor unimpressed with his rugged bed and breakfast accommodation, Omar was turned out into the coarse grass and reeds to the west of Cruach Cottage. Marc and I then spent the rest of the evening pouring over the maps. We carefully assessed the route, set up contingency meeting points and checked the GPS co-ordinates. Although crossing the moor by horse was a short distance of some twelve miles, it meant the best part of a one hundred mile detour for Marc. There was every possibility that given the lack of mobile telephone reception we would be out of contact for some time. So we brewed more tea, piled more logs on to the wood burning stove then checked the arrangements once more. In the late evening, we sweltered inside the cottage but the fire was the only means of heating water for the shower. As darkness began to fall, I crawled into my basic bed; fully aware that for a further night sleep would evade me. Typically, with the first real light bursting through the meagre curtains and the world slumbered, I rose with the silence of dawn.

Christine Thexton had given Iain clear instructions that we were not to leave until she arrived so we waited patiently. Omar had captivated Christine the minute she had met him the previous day. This kindly lady was determined that nothing was going to happen to her adopted horse so her instruction stood. At lunch the day before, Christine, Nick and Iain had poured over the plans for crossing the moor. We all sat around the big country table in their cottage at Rannoch Barracks near Bridge of Gaur, munching home made bread, cheese and ham and debated the options. I had prepared a contingency route that would take us over the "Road to the Isles", past Loch Ossian then on to Corrour and Roy Bridge but I wasn't entirely convinced that this much longer passage which would force us into a long northerly detour would be any better. Reports indicated that the incidence of soft peat laden terrain would deter progress as much as the direct route over the moor to the west. Nick confirmed that there were a number of very soft sections interspersed by deep ditches. So without the benefit of hindsight we continued with the original plan.

Omar was fed what appeared to be a miniscule breakfast. As a general rule horses should not be fed in anticipation of work, rather put back into them what has been taken out. Nevertheless feeding an endurance horse can be a complicated business. Horses in the wild spend about 16-20 hours of each day feeding. The gut has the actions of a trickle feeder - a small stomach and huge hindgut where bacteria ferments the food in a watery environment. They manage on fibre alone, choosing herbs to achieve a balanced diet. Riding horses are not any physiologically different and despite our artificial management at times need to be kept as near to the wild model as possible. A horse will eat 2-2.5% of its body weight per day of which at least 1% should be fibre. To sustain a moderate level of activity for long periods of time an endurance horse for example needs lots of water and electrolytes, body and brain fuel, the ability to keep cool and recover quickly. Although it seemed like a small amount of food, the balance was carefully calculated to provide exactly what would be needed.

Tacked up, impatient, ready to go Omar stood resplend-
ent in his black padded sheepskin girth and breastplate
ready for the arduous day that we knew, had planned for,
and would be ahead of us. Just how arduous that day was
to become hadn't quite been anticipated. But as they say,
even with the best-laid plans, along comes life! Already the
morning was starting to get warm, the mist on the high tops
burning off rapidly. Nick and Christine arrived in the pick
up, the Argocat lashed onto its back. We set off quickly into
the stillness of the forest, the only sound being the clatter
of the horse's shoes hitting the solid earth surface of the
track through the woods. As we trotted through the dense,
dark section of wood that runs parallel to the sweeping
length of Loch Laidon, the coolness was welcome. Pine
needles covered the track, muffling the sound of hooves.
The silence was deafening. Muscles now warmed up, we
walked, trotted, cantered. I focussed on the ride, trying
desperately hard not to think any further ahead than what
I could see immediately in front of me. But something
distracted me, caught my eye. The white and brown shape
was there again at my left side. It darted and weaved its
way in and out of the undergrowth, swinging through the
trees. This time I knew what it was, who it was. Instinctively
I knew that he would always be there, forever watching me,
staying by my side. I choked back a sob then laughed. As
we crossed the ford ten minutes later I was still smiling.

The transformation from forest to moor was starkly
evident and sobering. As we left the forest behind, the
vehicle with the Argocat went past. The track ahead rose
and fell into the barrenness. We climbed, descended then
climbed again. In the distance the Buachaille came into view.
I felt relaxed but an inner sense of apprehension still
pervaded. Each step was one more towards getting through
this desolate landscape. Only that thought temporarily

eased my consternation but with Nick, Christine and Iain I felt secure, safe in their concern and knowledge. Suddenly, the good track came to an end. From there the stark bleakness of moorland became reality. Ahead of me seemed miles of brown alien landscape broken only by the line of electric pylons on higher ground that march towards Kingshouse. I could just make out the faint mark of a path, extending beyond the turning point where Iain and Christine had unloaded the Argocat. In the near distance Buachaille Etive Mor with The Three Sisters beside him dominated the horizon but they still seemed a long way off. The small areas of plantation close to the Black Corries were in sight. We were close, but not close enough. Nick fired up the throaty engine then trailblazing a path they went off ahead of me. I relaxed but only slightly, safe in the knowledge, their knowledge, that I was secure. Then all too quickly they disappeared from sight. As soon as I took the first tentative steps on to the worst section of moor, suddenly, the sense of apprehension, trepidation and isolation washed over me. I was neither really afraid nor unduly worried but as I stepped forward, a voice rattled in my head - *This not an area to trifle with.* The ghost of Rannoch had me firmly in its grip.

Rannoch Moor is the watershed of Central Scotland although Nick Thexton has another phrase for it!! It is from here that the great rivers of Scotland are born to start their long journeys to the Atlantic in the west and North Sea in the east. It is a wild and sombre landscape, a terrifying wilderness covered in light coloured waving moor grasses, *molinia caerulea*, reeds and various hues of heather. For the more enthusiastic naturalist, the moor is home to the water lobelia *Lobelia dortmanna* and bulbous rush *Juncus bulbosus*. In addition this bleak expanse supports other uncommon species including least water lily *Nuphar pumila* and floating bur-reed *Sparganium angustifolium*. Rannoch Moor is a blanket bog that lies in a high level basin, standing at just under 350 metres above sea level. Its altitude is deceptive, surrounded as it is by the high tops of Glen Coe to the west, Leum Ulleim to the north, the hills of Perthshire and Schiehallion to the east. This is a world of shining lochans, black as night, sweeping lochs with tree clad islets and sandy bays. For its most part, the moor comprises of peat some 20-30 feet deep laid on granite. The entire area is scattered with thousands of enormous rocks and boulders, which have been torn from the hillsides and corries by a giant glacier some 20,000 years ago.

There is an abundance of bog myrtle or sweet gale, as it is commonly known. This is a sweet smelling plant with shallow roots that thrives on the peat-laden countryside; its existence testament to the obvious lack of drainage. The herb according to folklore is an effective source of midge repellent with anti-microbial and anti-bacterial properties, and once widely used in the more discerning aspects of culinary skills with chicken or fish. It was of particular interest to learn later of the myths that suggests it was from this plant that the Vikings brewed their legendary "berserk" potion, drunk before going into battle. Had I known that, I may well have sneaked out the night before to harvest some myself. Rannoch Moor is also home to the rare Rannoch Rush, *Scheuchzeria palustris,* a delicate little yellow green coloured plant grown nowhere else in Britain. This is also an ornithologists paradise with the trout populated lochans, sandy shores and islets providing a rich food source and residence to the goosander, black-throated diver and mer-ganser. On higher ground, eagles soar and with luck an osprey may be spotted. It is a fascinating place with an abundance of diverse interests generated by flora, fauna and human intervention. It can also be a terrifying location.

Although the moor generates a sense of wilderness in its purest sense, human interest and industrial demands are never far away. A line of electric pylons, some gently leaning over as the moor draws them ever downwards, march from Rannoch Station to the Black Corries as a permanent reminder of progress. Almost at right angles twisting like a drunken curve and cutting a swathe across the moorland in true railway modeller fashion is the inimitable West Highland Railway that bisects the moor.

This section of rail line from Tullich Station to Bridge of Orchy with its quaint unmanned and remote station stops at Rannoch and Corrour on which modern engines and carriages ply a regular overnight transport link from Mallaig to London Euston took some five thousand railway navvies nearly five years to build. The task was made almost impossible by the problem of peat and water. The peat had to be excavated, overlaid with brushwood, tree roots and thousands of tons of earth and ash so that a permanent way could be virtually floated across. But progress had its way, echoed in John Campbell Shairp's denouncement of the iron horses that were on the rampage through the Drumochter Pass in 1863.

Northwards still the iron horses!
Naught may stay their destined path
Till they snort by Pentland surges
Stun the cliffs of far Cape Wrath

It takes little imagination to realise the extent of the project and the hardships that the army of navvies had to endure. Lord Burton encouraged by the prospect of a fast journey to his sporting estate became a friend of the railway, supplying beer to overcome the brackish water available to the hard-pressed navvies. Apparently some modern travellers experience a distinct sense of seasickness as the carriages gently rise and fall on a line that virtually floats across the moor, somewhat akin to a vessel cutting through a gentle rolling swell. Just north of Rannoch Station itself the bog is some twenty feet deep and swallowed everything, thousands of tons of ballast that was thrown into it. It was here that one of the viaducts had to be constructed using Robert McAlpine, or "Concrete Bob's" new fangled mix. Progress was so slow at one point that the entire company ran out of money and the whole project was in jeopardy. James H Renton, Financial Director of the North British Railway Company gave part of his private fortune to save the situation. The railway navvies showed their gratitude by manhandling a huge boulder to nearby Rannoch station. From the stone they sculptured an excellent head of Mr Renton using nothing but the tools of their trade. The stone can be seen today on the north end of the station platform. The line, the greatest mileage of railway ever opened in the UK in one go made its debut on 11 ʰ August 1894 with the Mallaig extension some seven years later. An advertisement for a stationmaster at that time offered an annual salary of £60, a free house, coal, gas and the opportunity to be a notable figure in a small community.

In the same year that the West Highland Railway opened up the service from Glasgow to Fort William, the North British Aluminium Company was established with Lord Kelvin as technical adviser. As the first of the trains providing a regular transport link puffed and chuffed their black smoke and fiery embers onto the moor, just 12 miles west of the old Lubriadlach lodge, a further ambitious project was starting to take shape. It is here with the construction work that took place during the turn of the 20 ʰ century that the myth of Rannoch is also perpetuated. Local legend has it that a number of intoxicated navvies, fortified with strong ale from the pubs at Kinghouse disappeared into the peat hags as they attempted to stagger back over the Devil's Staircase to the camps that flourished near Kinlochleven during the construction of the Blackwater Dam. Of course in those days, someone missing from work in the morning was never an issue for the tough overseers that ruled the construction projects with thick leather belts backed up too often by a ready willingness to throw the odd jaw breaking punch.

As Loch Laidon linked to Loch Ba by the Abhainn Ba provides an efficient barrier against any immediate escape off the moor to the south, the Blackwater Reservoir dominates the area to the north. The water from Laidon drains towards Loch Eigheach then onwards to the great hydro dams of Rannoch and Tummel and eventually the North Sea. From the hills to the north above Loch Laidon a converse action is in place. Draining from Loch Claidheimh and desolate Loch Chiarinn, the Black Water and Ciaran rivers pour a constant supply of water into a hungry man made reservoir some thirteen kilometres in length, the construction of which flooded out the last inhabitants of the area at the tail end of the 19[h] Century. From there the waters from Rannoch eventually find their way to the Atlantic. The memories of the population that eked a living from the harsh countryside are echoed as elsewhere by Professor Shairp's haunting thoughts:

"By the wee birchen corries lie patches of green,
Where gardens and bareheaded bairnies have been
But the huts now are rickles of stones nettle grown
And the once human homes, e'en their names are unknown."

The old drovers road that would have taken travellers southwest from the peripheries of the Monadhliath follows its way along the Alt Fheith Chiarinn past Loch Chiarinn then the Alt an Inbhir to join up with the Blackwater at its western extremity. Towards the confluence of the river there stands a monument in the shape of a Celtic cross. This commemorates a drowning, perhaps a hapless drover. The dam, almost a thousand metres long was constructed in 1904 using an early type of concrete, not smooth like its modern counterpart but filled with pebbles and stones. In its time this was one of the worlds greatest feats of civil engineering.

The construction work of the dam that created the Blackwater Reservoir is probably best told in the brilliant book *"The Children of the Dead End"* by Irish navvy turned writer Patrick McGill. It is a tale of the harsh living conditions and brutality that epitomised the life of itinerate labourers at the turn of the 20 [h] century. In testimony to the harshness of the work and unforgiving nature of the conditions that prevailed at that time, there is at the base of the dam atop a small hillock a graveyard within which the headstones are carved of the same rough concrete. Mostly these depict Irish or Highland names, but many are simply scratched as "Unknown". There is also the grave of one solitary woman. What she was doing there amidst a couple of thousand men is anyone's guess. Perhaps she did the laundry?

And now, at another, later point in time, a few miles east of that makeshift graveyard, Team Omar became locked in a different battle of hardship. As Omar sank a few inches down into another boggy section, small lumps of wet peat were splattered through the air. I spat the dirt from my mouth; wiped the ooze from my eyes. The saddle was splashed with orangey brown iron impregnated water and mud. Omar was covered from belly to rump in the stuff. I was saturated from boots to thighs in the orange muck. We pushed on but it was hard.

Splash!

Squelch!

It was very tough going. The Argocat disappeared from view over the next rise, tyre tracks instantly obliterated. Should I go low to my left or work slightly higher to the right? I go right but it's the wrong decision. We sink down again, squelching into the ooze.

I am almost ready to call this a day, not prepared under any circumstances to put an ego before my horse. We pushed on through the peat, picking our way carefully, cautiously, trying to identify solid ground. But it was deceptive, even the dry looking grass patches were wet and boggy. There was sphagnum moss everywhere blasting out a warning to stay away. Immediately under the heather there is nothing compact, just the glint of running water. A bit further and the dark green Argocat came into view. Christine looked anxiously back for us. Nick and Iain are willing us on. We plod on towards them. Again I go too high and again we sink. But this time the ground is getting firmer. Alongside of us the electric pylons are bending to the north, with them the track is rising gently on to more solid ground The Buachaille is getting closer, almost touching distance away. The first flash of white paint on the Kingshouse belies the distance. Vehicles can be seen running along the A82 at the foot of the Buachaille. Relief? No this is not a time or place to relax. Every ounce of my being is lost in concentration. Physical strength is ebbing fast, sweat pouring off me. I have no concept of time but try to will the horse on. Then another ditch - we jump clear.

Squelch!

Splash!

As Omar lands he sinks again but this time its not so deep. As he kicks out splashing peat and water there is a dull thud. Instinctively I knew that something was wrong. Worried, I check his legs but everything is fine. I lifted his feet one at a time then discover that the offside foreleg shoe is damaged and bent. It is likely that the edge of the shoe caught a stone or root, the deep ooze acting as suction. It needed to come off. With only fifty metres to cover before reaching the hard firm track, the worst-case scenario had occurred and it couldn't have happened in a more desolate place.

Within minutes Christine, Nick and Iain are around us. With one shoe now bent, Omar cannot be moved anywhere through the boggy ground but is calm as we focus all our attention on trying to get the twisted shoe off. I didn't feel any sense of disappointment, my sole concern being Omar and how to get him off that inhospitable watershed. The toolkit in my bum bag is woefully inadequate for the purpose, nothing in the Argocat suitable. For a short while the air buzzed with mobile telephone calls as Iain contacts Marc immediately diverting him from the long haul around to the next stage point at Kingshouse. Christine called her son Gregor who was quickly on his way with pinchers and heavier tools. I was humbled by the fact that offers of assistance poured in from people all along Rannoch. I saw the look of disappointment and dejection in their faces and I wanted to hug them all.

Then after standing helpless for what seemed like hours Nick succeeded in getting the damaged shoe off. I checked Omar again, breathing a sigh of relief when an inspection shows that there is no noticeable damage to his hoof. We were beyond the point of no return but started to retreat slowly over the moor. It was like fighting a rear guard action as we retraced our steps. Omar stayed calm, crunching on the Polo mint I give him as a treat. As usual he was totally untroubled, unfazed by the excitement. But today there was no going on. What earlier seemed like touching distance to success started to fade into the distance as failure reared its ugly face. I turned but don't look back. For me, I felt nothing except relief that my horse was safe and well.

The extraction from the moor took a long time. Ironically, the one redeeming quality was the soft terrain that prevented any sustained pressure or damage to the unprotected hoof. It was a slow process but gradually we inched our way back. I removed the saddle and breastplate to allow Omar some better freedom of movement as together; side-by-side we jumped ditches and boggy sections. The bridle and bit with the reins attached was left in place. This way I had better control if I really needed it but our retreating actions became a well-rehearsed routine. We would stop before each obstacle; catch our breath then together we leapt across, as often as not landing with a splash or splattering of wet peaty ooze. On the other side, we stopped to relax. I patted and fussed over Omar, encouraging him each step of the way. The others watched in fascination at this ultimate bond between man and horse. Each step was a committed act of faith, total trust. Where I led, he followed. I was very proud. The legend of *An Duine Mor*, The Big Man or Husband, the ghostly figure that appears and guides stranded travellers off the moor to safety didn't quite materialise but I am sure his presence was all pervading.

Slowly we made it back to the hard packed ground at the turning circle to await Marc whom at that time was negotiating a very difficult tree lined track. With only inches to spare from the ditches that guarded each side of the access road Marc eased the Land Rover and trailer slowly along. As we waited patiently, the considerate ever practical

Christine fed us her homemade bread, ham and cheese sandwiches, which were washed down with coffee from the flasks. Eventually Marc, surprised by the distance we had covered in such a short time arrived with the trailer. Omar was loaded without fuss then slowly we drove him back over the bouncing forest track and fords to the paddock at Cruach Cottage.

The rest of the day was a whirlwind of decision making, frantic telephone calls to arrange a farrier and newspaper interviews. Marc had been caught unawares by a telephone call from one newspaper and had naively stated that we were stuck in the middle of nowhere. I was more concerned that someone may well have found a story that didn't really exist. I don't like dealing with the media and have a distinct lack of mistrust. Some days later, when I eventually read the article that had been written after the arrival at Mar Lodge, the content, overstated and factually incorrect both shocked and disgusted me. My sense of distrust was justified. The photograph that accompanied the article depicted prima facie an exhausted and stern looking rider. Apparently slumped over his horse. But I suppose as Chateaubriand once said *"The more serious the face, the more beautiful the smile."* Five minutes previously we had trotted proudly past the building, wet, dishevelled maybe but with a broad grin, the radiance burning inside me. That would have made a much better representation. Nevertheless, by late afternoon, any sense of abrupt media castigation had subsided, the press correctly briefed that we had lost the shoe and were now taking steps to redress the unfortunate situation. Our immediate logistics had been swiftly re-arranged, a farrier organised. We even had time to relax, basking in the hot sun. As walkers from The Great Outdoors Challenge passed by, Omar, thriving on the attention, was checked over and cleaned up. The peat that had hardened on his legs was washed off but the orange stains from the heavy iron content endured for days to come. Brushed and groomed all over, he was rugged up then fed his evening meal and supplements, seemingly bearing no side effects. Indeed when released into the paddock he immediately cantered off to visit the two sheep and hens that he had accepted as his new albeit temporary stable mates. We watched fascinated as Omar, intent on impressing us with his healthy prowess pranced around the paddock in true Arabian style - tail erect, mane flowing, head held high in pride.

The loss of the shoe was a blow but not catastrophic. It did however leave me with a number of options, all of which of course hinged around conformation from Neil Chalmers, the farrier, that there was no immediate hoof issues that would prevent us from continuing. Realistically, since we were to meet Neil at Killiecrankie the next morning, it would be time consuming and impractical to drive back to Rannoch then start all over again. Anyway, the experience on that section of the moor was more than enough so that was discounted.

Option two was to return to Loch Eigheach then head up the "Road to the Isles" and hence Fort William by way of old Lubriadlach Lodge, Loch Ossian and Corrour. This would mean a huge northerly detour and I was desperate to get back onto a route where I could keep a direct westerly heading. Although the route that leads past Ossian had been prepared, mapped and logged to the GPS as a contingency, in terms of accommodation for Omar, we would still be in unplanned logistics.

Although I was confident that we probably would be able to find a make do paddock for the night, I didn't like the idea of just turning up unannounced. Even so, the thought of plodding through areas of potentially peat saturated ground again sent shivers through me, especially after some heavy rain was forecast for that night. As it turned out, the forecast was correct. The third option was therefore the most obvious. In practical terms, all we really had to do was drive around to Kingshouse, pick up the moor near the Black Corries where we left off and continue from there. So that was decided.

After a very early morning start, we drove the slow twisting thirty-five miles from Rannoch Station to the Killiecrankie Visitor Centre where Neil was waiting for us. As he worked on Omar's new shoes, the National Trust staff busied around in the early morning preparation for a new day of tourism. A horse being shod in their car park was a new experience for them. A horse in the car park full stop was novel enough. So the manager, intent in finding material suitable for the NTS Newsletter rushed off to get her camera. As she returned, marching towards Omar, camera at the ready he spotted the possibility of media stardom then decided that it seemed an appropriate time to display the full extent of his albeit restricted manhood. Embarrassed by this sudden, unexpected hint of exhibition-ism she stopped dead in her tracks, blushed a reasonable level of red in the process, and then hesitated in taking any further steps forward. Marc, spotting the situation, quickly saved the day by pulling the turn out rug down far enough to allow a more modest picture to be taken for the NTS Newsletter. Why this photogenic horse performs this embarrassing act every time someone appears with a camera is anyone's guess? Very reluctantly I also dispelled the implied suggestion that I was in fact Prince Omar. The other young woman who had proffered the question did actually seem quite disappointed at the reply. Impervious to the amusement that was taking place around him Neil busied himself with Omar's feet. By 9:30am the farrier work was completed. Old shoes were off, feet trimmed and a new set of gleaming steel perfectly fitted.

We thanked Neil, bid our goodbyes to the National Trust staff, loaded Omar back into the trailer then set off for Kingshouse and the Black Corries by way of Aberfeldy, Killin and Tyndrum. As we settled into the comparatively short distance of 80 miles, our minds focussed on one thing - finding somewhere for a late breakfast. As luck would have it, the only available place we could find was something akin to Ye Olde Bake House in Killin. Or perhaps it was more similar to Mrs Miggin's Pie Shop in the Blackadder television series. Now whether the husband and wife owners were just having a bad day that morning or hated each other's presence at all times or they were just naturally inhospitable was enough for me to walk out in disgust. I was sorely tempted to hurtle abuse back at the rudeness displayed but sheer greed for the bacon sandwich – without sauce please - kept me firmly in check. What did spring to mind was some of the opening lines from Charlene's recently revamped song:

> *"Hey lady. You lady. Cursing at your life.*
> *You're a discontented mother and a regimented wife.*
> *I have no doubt you dream about.*
> *The things you'll never do."*

As we munched the rolls, washed down with an unique blend of "coffee" Marc put forward his new found theory that somewhere along the middle of Rannoch Moor, dividing north and south there is a discreet communications system that switches off people's personality and their sense of humour. It was an interesting thought and as we were to find out later, it began to seem like a reasonably accurate hypothesis. We hastened on for the Black Corries and the western side of Rannoch Moor, ever watchful for the tell tale signs of unusual telecommunications activity that might render the human being with a set of permanent dysfunctional characteristics. As temperatures gradually warmed a day that became increasingly hotter, Team Omar were back in action but heading for a showdown near a lonely outpost below the Buachaille Etive Mor.

Pilgrims in the Sun

*"We are the Pilgrims Master; we shall go
always a little further."*

I F the arrival at Blair Atholl had proved to be a significant
milestone, the section involving the tussle with the Moor
of Rannoch had been by comparison a major hurdle. It
had been a bold yet calculated attempt to cross the shortest
section of moor from east to west but circumstances dictated
otherwise. We were of course disappointed but strangely
enough there was no real sense of failure. The risks had
been high and we had lost. But the sheer experience in
following in the wake rather than footsteps of proud
pioneering people whose unwitting contributions to the
historical nature of the area had been more than a privilege.
That fact far outweighed any sense of loss. It had been a
punch-up with nature in a notorious area and nature won.
Reluctantly that compromise to a battle lost was acceptable.
Now we had to move on. Because now the task at hand was
to pick up where we had left off then head onwards towards
the old cattle stance that the drovers used near Altnafeadh
and the climb into the notorious Devils Staircase.

Rannoch Moor, "that thorofare of thieves", as it was once
described is a disconsolate place but an amazing area. The
route westward across the moor from Rannoch Station was
never a popular thoroughfare. As an alternative, the drovers
heading from the peripheries of the Monaliath range

headed south via Corrour then along the edge of what is now the Blackwater Reservoir. On the eastern edge of the moor, cattle were herded from Skye and Fort William south towards the great Trysts at Falkirk and Crieff. From the south, Wade's shovelling brigades marched their coarse roads northwards and two thousand miles of military road set the foundations for Scotland's modern road system. And it was over those roads that the engineers, labourers and industrialists came as development slowly but gradually moved into the western highlands. It was inevitable then that eventually our path was destined to cross with that of the old drovers, soldiers, Irish navvies, pedlars, brigands, bandits, rustlers and travellers of every sort. Where history converged was at a lonely outpost under the shadow of the Buachaille Etive Mor and known as the Kingshouse Hotel.

According to A R B Haldane, writing in *The Drove Roads of Scotland*, the passing of the eighteenth century saw very little change in the standard of accommodation provided for the wayfarer. At the end of the century, travellers from the south coming to Scotland in ever increasing numbers all had the same complaint. Many of the inns of the highlands of this period were still only wayside cottages, providing little more than the rough spirit, illicitly distilled. With this and the small black cattle, and the sea kelp of the islands and coastal districts, these were the only products that the highlanders of the time could eke out their meagre livelihood. Kingshouse Inn on the Moor of Rannoch was a key point on the drove roads that led the drovers south to the Falkirk or Crieff trysts. Here the need for an inn and the lack of incentive to keep one was recognised by the government of the day. Travellers of the eighteenth and early nineteenth centuries record that the innkeeper sat rent-free and received an annual government grant. Despite this, the description of the place was bleak. Travellers during the droving periods show the inn to have been a rough and cheerless place. One wayfarer of 1791 described the King-shouse as not having a bed fit for a decent person to sleep in, nor any provisions but what are absolutely necessary for the family. In 1802, James Donaldson, Surveyor of the Military Roads complained that it "has more of an appear-ance of a hog stye than an Inn." Dorothy Wordsworth went even further the following year with her comments in that "Never did I see such a miserable such wretched place – as dirty as a house after a sale on a rainy day." Obviously Dorothy wasn't a great fan of her stay at the Kingshouse and went on to say, " - long rooms with ranges of beds, no other furniture except benches, or perhaps one or two crazy chairs, the floors far dirtier than an ordinary house could be if it were never washed. With length of time the fire was kindled and after another hour of waiting, supper came, a shoulder of mutton so hard that it was impossible to chew the little flesh that might have been scraped off the bones."

The Kingshouse Hotel is a remote inn and hotel at the eastern end of Glen Coe at the junction with Glen Etive. It is sited in an isolated position about two kilometers to the east of the Buachaille Etive Mor, a dramatic peak of almost Alpine characteristics. The property lies on the old military Wade road over Rannoch Moor which now forms the West Highland Way and crosses the River Etive at the hotel before continuing into the glen and ascending the Devil's Staircase before crossing the hills towards Kinlochleven. Built in the 17 ʰ century, the hotel is thought to be one of Scotland's oldest licensed inns. After the battle of Culloden in 1746, the building became a barracks for troops of King George III engaged in crushing the last vestiges of Jaco-bitism, thus getting the name King's House.

By 1903, standards had changed and Alexander Wilkie recorded that "arriving at King's House I have a hearty welcome. Tea, my clothes and shoes dried. Next morning after a walk round I go for breakfast. What shall I have? – Grapefruit? What! Can I have grapefruit in King's House, of course I can, and so I have grapefruit and porridge and cream and fish and everything just like a west end city. I tell you I am well looked after and at a charge so moderate that I am almost shamed of my appetite."

Maybe that is why the early drovers preferred the option of staying outside, enduring the elements instead. But these were a different breed altogether. Many drovers remained true to their calling and their traditions resting at night with their cattle. Wrapped in their heavy plaids on which the frost showed white or the dew shone bright just as it does on a spider's web. Their sticks near their hands, they slumbered peacefully. In a striking similarity to pioneers across the international domain, Sir John Sinclair said in his Analysis of the Statistical Account of Scotland, "He has felt from his early youth, all the privations to which he can be exposed in almost any circumstances of war. He has been accustomed to scanty fare, to rude and often wet clothing, to cold and damp houses, to sleep often in the open air or in the most uncomfortable beds, to cross dangerous rivers, to march a number of miles without stopping and with but little nourishment, and to be perpetually exposed to the attacks of a stormy atmosphere. A warrior thus trained, suffers no inconvenience from what others would consider to be the greatest possible hardships, and has an evident superiority over the native of a delicious climate, bred to every indulgence of food, dress and habitation and who is unaccustomed to marching and fatigue." Quite possibly some endurance riders will identify with that! Faced with their arduous bleak journey across the moor, I felt more than just a hint of compassion as we prepared once again to do battle with Rannoch Moor.

The path leading from the section of Rannoch Moor close to the Tigh na Cruaiche, becomes increasingly firmer as it bends towards the Black Corries. As the route begins to climb gently on to higher levels, skirting the wetter, boggy ground adjacent to Loch Laidon, the gentle gradient allows more natural drainage to take place. This ensures that the path stays reasonably dry, the conditions much more conducive to easier transit. By the time the swirling burns of Alt Riabhach Mor and Alt Riabhach a Chinn Tuill had been crossed, the worst of the moor firmly over, the ground harder, rockier in places. From the gentle terrain that rises and falls in quick succession the aspects of civilization never seem to be far away. In the near distance the Black Corries Lodge is constantly in view just beyond small forestry plantations and behind them, the white painted aspect of the Kingshouse Hotel. By the time the Alt Dubh Mor is crossed, the narrow constrictive pathway gives way to a wider firm estate road, adorned with rickety wooden bridges. From the Black Corries Lodge to the hotel and the intersection with the West Highland Way is a mere three kilometers.

Our sojourn at the Kingshouse was as brief as possible. If the travellers of the previous centuries had found this to be an inhospitable place, our experience was quite the opposite. The lengthy day, allied to the increasing heat from a bright sun in a cloudless blue sky induced a growing sense of lethargy. The walkers sipping cool beer, sitting outside at trestle tables induced a sense of envy. In search of the toilets I walked into the hotel and in doing so bumped into the kindly owner, Kitty Leach at the reception desk. When I explained what we were doing and why she had a horse tethered just outside the front door, the proprietor could not have been more welcoming or hospitable. Within a few minutes, Kitty appeared beside Omar, a kindly retainer at hand carrying a silver service tray, coffee pot, cups, saucers, milk jug and sugar bowl. The tray was also festooned with an assortment of biscuits. Had I requested grapefruit, I would probably have got that too! Refreshments were on the house. I thanked them profusely then managed to dissuade Kitty from letting Omar into her adjacent garden for a "rest". Her member of staff went off to get a camera instead. By that point Omar was the subject of growing interest, sufficiently enough for a throng of people to gather around, cameras at the ready. Some expressed an interest in stroking him. Of course by now we knew what happens when Omar comes into contact with camera wielding, admiring crowds. Just as the elderly member of staff returned, camera at the ready, his lordship once again decided to impress the crowd with his exhibitionist peculiarity. This time there was no rug to pull down to deny embarrassment. For a mere second, I quite firmly believed that we could well have had at least one fainting casualty on our hands. It was definitely cue to leave. Exit a quick stage right.

To the south side of the hotel, lies the old humpbacked stone bridge constructed by General George Wade's battalion of shovelling soldiers as the military road was carved towards Kinlochleven. Below the bridge, the River Etive gurgled, its waters refreshed by the last of the snowmelt that fed its tributaries from the slopes of Meall Bhalach and Beinn a Chrulaiste. As we crossed the bridge, the sound of iron shoes clattering in the still afternoon seemed to generate a feeling of the history that surrounds the inn. Briefly I imagined the government troops, bright red jackets, canvas webbing blancoed brilliant white, and officers on horseback, marching into the hills in perfect order.

Once across the bridge, I swung left on to the old single-track road that leads from the back of the hotel to join up with the track to the Black Corries. As I did so, I glanced quickly behind me to look back over the openness of the last section of Rannoch Moor. For a fleeting moment I could just make out the trees at the opposite end but from now on in, we moved on to firmer albeit steeper terrain, free from the deep, water soaked, peat laden ground. Close to where the single-track road from the hotel meets the busy A82, the marker posts, engraved in their wood indicating the West Highland Way were clearly evident. As I turned Omar right onto the narrow footpath then through the first gate, I noted with a sense of alarm that there were a number of pedestrian stiles in the immediate distance ahead of me. Something didn't seem correct. I was right to be concerned.

Inevitably they came. Footsore weary devotees heading for their own temple of personal fulfilment, they traipsed their way north along the acrid dusty paths. Some came in small groups, others singly. Some were friendly; others I suppose were a bit like me, reserved, focussed on what they were doing with no real time for idle chat. Apparently, each year some 85,000 people use the West Highland Way, traditionally walking the 92-mile route from Milngavie to Fort William. This direction of travel has a purpose. It means that the walkers have the sun on their backs all day. Whatever! So as we worked our way up on to the higher ground on the side of Beinn a Chrulaiste and Stob Beinn a Chrulaiste, we either had walkers directly ahead or those following on from behind. Occasionally we did meet some casual day hikers going from the Kingshouse to Altnafeadh and back or vice versa. As the track is quite narrow, the walkers generally gave us a wide berth, although on more than one occasion it was manifestly obvious from the looks of contempt that this was a route sacrosanct for walkers, the horse an intruder.

But the West Highland Way, like so many modern reconstructions is not a wilderness track. In fact it is quite the opposite. It is perfectly feasible that a walker could start at whichever end then reach the other point without recourse to a map. Such is the elaborate nature of the well-marked trail, amply adorned with the plethora of sign posts engraved with the hallmark thistle. Everything on the West Highland Way is for walkers and everything is there to prevent them getting their feet wet, losing direction or catching their clothes on the edges of barbed wire fences. A wilderness trail it most certainly isn't.

But by the time we reached the end of the first climb onto the slopes of Stob Beinn a Chrulaiste, I sensed we were heading for trouble. The gates I had to open were not a real issue as the obligatory pedestrian steps over the fences acted as very useful mounting blocks. What did bother me was the narrow wooden boardwalks and strategically placed stepping-stones that bridged the overabundance of small streams and burns that tinkled off the steep hillside. Just as I had manoeuvred Lady past similar flagstones over water near Jocks Road, Omar had to be carefully coaxed into the mud and peat in order to bypass the obstacles. Given his experience in the peat hags of Rannoch, he was understandably none too fond of black shiny peat or mud and water. Thankfully, we worked our way over the water obstacles without any real problem. With the exception of opening and closing gates, I did not have to dismount to lead him over anything that he initially hesitated at, curiosity merely stopping him momentarily as he took stock of the situation. That was perfectly acceptable. At each narrow wooden boardwalk or mini-bridge we walked slowly, cautiously, carefully, just taking our time.

Gradually, we commenced our descent, in doing so started closing with the main road where the West Highland Way runs parallel and very adjacent to the A82, the notorious Glasgow to Fort William route. From a vantage point on the highest section of track I paused to look down on the busy road. Cars, buses, motorcycles, articulated trucks and even the occasional slow moving cyclist could be seen. The traffic speed seemed horrendous. What amazed me even more was the evident heat rising from the black tarmac. It was a very hot afternoon, the temperature somewhere near 30 degrees centigrade; the road surface almost appeared to be melting. For the first time I also noticed the overpowering stench of fumes held in the airless depth of the valley. On the left the Buachaille Etive Mor stood out crystal clear in the warm afternoon sun, the last vestiges of snow remained on the summit ridge, still held in the deep ravines and gullies. The sky was virtually cloudless, the air stagnant in the glen, the temperature rose. The stench of artificiality beckoned, I groaned, again!

Ahead of me I could just make out the rusty red corrugated roofs of the steadings at Altnafeadh, just above them the start of the Devil's Staircase. To the left of that but on the other side of the road, the Scottish Mountaineering Club's hut at Laggangarbh could be seen, its whitewashed walls glinting in the bright sunlight. Marc was waiting there. As we closed on the main road, the West Highland Way, now separated from the main road by just a few metres of rough ground and a ditch, started to run parallel with the A82. Dismounting to open an additional gate, I was about to climb back into the saddle, then spotted what I thought was another gate about a hundred metres ahead of me. The pedestrian stile could be clearly seen and I assumed, incorrectly as it turned out, that there would be a gate beside it. So instead of re-mounting, I walked Omar along the last bit of path. As I reached the stile, I stood flabbergasted – there was no gate but what was there was a fence, a barbed wire stock fence running right across the West Highland Way. Someone, somewhere had made a mistake. Hastily I called Marc on the UHF. Within a few minutes he arrived, walking the few hundred metres from the vehicle at Laggangarbh.

As try as we might, there was no way around this obstacle. In frustration, I kicked the fence posts, which were only held in place by the strands of wire, the points in the ground, rotted through. Some of the walkers, who caught up with us, each gave the posts a hearty kick but their efforts were too no avail. Their condemnation of fenced off pathways was unconcealed, their sympathy for my plight generous. There was nothing we could do. I was furious. Marc stayed cool. Omar chomped at the sparse grass by the stile, totally indifferent to the situation, but as I rested my hands on my head in despair, he turned to look at me, seemingly offering his sympathy. For a few more minutes we assessed the situation. We certainly couldn't get over the stock fence. The option of crossing the main road or leading along the edge of a busy thoroughfare was far too risky. Anyway at each side of the road there were a number of drainage ditches, the ground that could be seen, deep, wet and boggy. Anger gave way to frustration, frustration to disappointment then eventually I resigned myself to the fact that we would have to do a complete about turn and head all the way back to Kingshouse then trailer Omar along to Altnafeadh. As it turned out there was one further gate just ahead – and that was well and truly secured by padlock and chain. Why a locked gate was there in the first place seems to indicate a pretty shoddy standard of estate management. Nevertheless, for the second day in succession we were beating a fighting retreat. Time was marching on. We had no other option.

In the course of planning the route for the Trans Scotland, each and every landowner or estate, without exception was contacted by letter or e-mail. The reasons for this were quite simple – to avoid the sort of situation we were now in. Clearly, if our proposed route involved sections where locked gates or fences or insecure bridges existed, we needed to know well in advance. Not asking for favours, what we did was common courtesy. Yet, despite the provisions of the Land Reform Act and access rights to the country at large there are still many landowners or specifically their appointed agents or employees who remain deliberately obstinate or downright un-cooperative when it comes to access. It would be easy to launch into a criticism of modern day Scottish landownership and the associated anachronistic forms of estate management but that can wait because in fairness not all landowners or their management lie at the bottom levels of competence. Up to that point, the co-operation and generosity displayed by all the estates that we had crossed were second to none! The old drove roads were utilised on a regular basis with access enshrined in common law. As far I am aware, that access has never been revoked. Therefore blocking right of entry would contradict the principles of establishment. Someone with the where-withal is all that is needed to continue to challenge the ignorance that prevails.

Turning Omar to head back to the first gate, my boot slipped off the edge of a boardwalk. Following obediently behind me, he too skidded off the wooden planks, slipped into the narrow ditch alongside, inadvertently running his leg down the jagged edge of the wooden boards. Omar leapt up, kicking out with a gashed foreleg, the wound clearly evident. For a minute or so, he stretched and kicked out his damaged leg, seemingly shaking off the stinging pain. Within a couple of minutes he settled down. I was devastated, furious. Concerned for my horse, I quickly examined the wound then realised that although the cut looked quite long and deep, it was more superficial. At the next burn I splashed cold water on to the graze, using my gloves to wipe down the wound. He didn't flinch once. I remained infuriated, inevitable then that the first people I came across were going to feel my wrath. As it turns out, the three elderly walkers that we met were kind, sympathetic and equally contemptuous of the fact that someone had placed an obstacle across the path. Effectively, as they reasoned, such an obstacle restricted the West Highland Way for horses. Their condemnation of Scottish landowners or in this case their employees were equally fierce. As one hill walker at the behest of his wife, rummaged in his hefty rucksack for an apple, I chatted to the others who were all over Omar with sympathy. As the horse chomped on his welcome apple, I calmed down, at least momentarily. With the three hikers heading on their way to Fort William, I called Marc on the radio to pass on the fact that Omar was injured and that we would be taking our time.

For the next hour we plodded back along the track, passing numerous walkers along the way, neither of who exchanged much in the way of passing pleasantries. Perhaps the anti-personality-counter-sense-of-humour mast was working again. Most certainly I was I no mood for idle chitchat. Gradually, slowly we worked our way back up on to the high point, just taking our time avoiding any wet ground. Despite the fact that the day lingered on in hot glorious sunshine, I lost all sense of the surroundings, my focus of concentration was Omar, the path directly ahead. Nothing more. Before starting the descent, I checked Omar's leg. If anything the wound appeared to have dried up – a good sign. There was no lameness. In fact he seemed none too fazed, typically indifferent to the whole situation. A true pro! But inside me I seethed with a festering sense of anger ready to be directed at the person, whether inadvertently or not, was responsible for the injury to my horse. This one incident ensured that I was neither about to forgive nor forget.

As fate would have it, as we reached the start of the track to the Black Corries Lodge, there working on fences, stripped to the waist in the hot sun, a walking example apathetic to Health and Safety issues, was whom I perceived to be the "estate manager". In the ensuing fracas that developed, in full view of passing walkers and tourists, this example of indifference, a product of absentee landownership stood no chance of success. The verbal onslaught that I subjected him to was merciless. Despite us having written to the estate outlining the route and asking for comments, he initially denied the existence of the stock wire, denied the existence of a locked gate. But when I called Marc over to show him the photographs we had taken on the digital camera, he backed off then miraculously remembered where those were!

"You'll be taking the matter further will you, " he smirked at me.

"Oh, you better believe that, " I replied.

Whether he sensed the punch that was close to arriving at any given minute or the kick that might just be coming from Omar as I backed towards him, he retreated. Whichever action he feared was on its way, he called for his son to his side, and then in a truly subservient manner, he withdrew. Quickly! As I crossed the Wade Bridge with Omar, I swear that the horse gave out a chuckle. I smiled broadly.

The entire incident with the fence and the altercation left me with a sour taste. I wanted away from the place. Back at the hotel we checked Omar's leg again, applying some antiseptic gel to the gash. He certainly didn't seem any the worst for the cut. There were no signs of lameness, no swelling. On the contrary, the wound appeared to have commenced the healing process quite rapidly. Fortunately, the remaining part of the ride would keep us away from any further wet or boggy ground. That at least ensured that the wound would stay dry, free from any infection. As passers-by bustled around, we loaded Omar into the trailer then departed the Kingshouse as fast as possible.

From Altnafeadh the ubiquitous signpost indicates the West Highland Way route to Kinlochleven, continuing over perhaps its most spectacular section. This is the famous, or for some, iniquitous Devil's Staircase. It was here that General Wade's engineering soldiers cut and carved their way in sharp twisting turns, up the side of Stob Mhic Mhartuin. Understandably, carrying materials up that stretch of road was never a popular assignment. From the roadside, just beyond the small copse of trees, where only a steel barrier separates the path from the busy A82, the track ahead is clear, looks steep, rocky and imposing. For the walkers intent in concluding the West Highland Way this is a major hurdle after many days of traipsing along comparatively flat or gentle undulating ground. For a capable endurance horse that thrives on steep rocky climbing, the ascent is nothing more than another manageable challenge. From Altnafeadh the immediate climb zigzags its way in fewer than three hundred metres to a high point. This makes the ascent seem steep. In fact looking up, it could be construed as almost vertical in places. But these roads were designed for shifting military wagons and armaments by horse, even passenger carriages. From the highest point the view back to Altnafeadh and Glen Coe is stunning, the sense of altitude very apparent. The route then winds its way gently downhill through the more open moor land that lies between Beinn Bheag and Stob Mhic Mhartuin then the Sron a Choire Odhair Bhig.

Once the Alt na Choire Odhair Bhig burn has been crossed, the descent is more noticeable. For the final three kilometres the Old Military Road meanders its way downwards until it reaches the dam road at the pumping station where the pipes to the smelter started the build up for the turbines in the generating station. Still quite steep, the road continues towards Kinlochleven until eventually it passes through the woods, past the old aluminium works then onwards to the tail race where the water rushes out, finally coming to an end at the village itself. From Altnafeadh to Kinlochleven the distance is a mere eight kilometres but that belies an awful lot of hard work and sheer effort. For the navvies who walked over this hill path to blow their sub in the Kingshouse then staggered back to their camps, I had nothing but admiration. On a cold winter's night the devil often claimed his own.

The history of Kinlochleven, the village that sits at the end of Loch Leven is mottled. According to our old friend Thomas Pennant, as he passed through on his travels across Scotland, there was once an inn here in the 18[h] century where he breakfasted on minced stag. Today there is more than an inn, the village was built as a small "new town" to serve the aluminium works and consists of a number of blocks of 2-storey houses. These are very much in the form of a "model-village" style common to the period. With a steady influx of labour, Kinlochleven flourished. Some may describe it as a nice place. I wouldn't. Interestingly though as I looked down into the cluster of houses and hotels from the high hillside, for a fleeting moment I could imagine a similarity to an Alpine location, the backdrop of hills beyond creating that impression. On the north side of the village, the mighty Mamores range, with Ben Nevis behind them, dominated the skyline. But the real giveaway to its birth and history of industrialism are the abandoned works and the massive water carrying pipes that proliferate the hillsides.

It was close to here in 1904 that the Blackwater Dam was constructed. In the same year an Act of Parliament established the Loch Leven Water and Electric Power Company, which merged with the North British Aluminium Company Limited. A new business of producing the light metal using electrolysis required vast levels of power. The prodigious rainfall of the west coast and its mountain topography made perfect partners for the enterprising project. The water to drive the turbines was provided by the Blackwater Dam, which in its heyday had a capacity when full of running the smelter for eighty days. Approximately five years later, the aluminium smelter works opened. When in production, the Kinlochleven plant was at one time the smallest and oldest smelter in the world, specialising in high purity aluminium. At the turn of the millennium, the plant was closed. Most of the factory was demolished while some parts of the complex were retained for alternative uses. The carbon silos/bunkers, vast arcaded rubble blocks incorporating structures of early reinforced concrete were converted for the Kinlochleven Development Trust as an outdoor activity centre and microbrewery. But nowadays, Kinlochleven sits back and basks in the pilgrimage of the West Highland Way, the steady stream of visitors and tourists that this brings.

But our day was not to end at Kinlochleven. From there we had a steady climb up past the Mamore Lodge Hotel to George and Mags Loudon's cottage and Omar's overnight accommodation. As Mags fed us mugs of coffee we set about a more thorough examination of Omar's leg. The wound was still raw but didn't seem anywhere as bad as I had first imagined. Chomping on his hay net, he stood absolutely still as the wound and surrounding areas of skin were cleaned. A liberal coating of herbal antiseptic gel was applied; a gauze pad then a generous overlay of stretchy veterinary wrap to finish off the bandaging. As usual he remained utterly unfazed. With his hard feed inside him, his turn out rug in place, sprayed amply with insect repellent, I led him up the track to the paddock that Geordie said was through the gates "just" past the wooden bridge. About one and a half kilometres later, I reached the open hillside, exhausted and hanging on to Omar's neck for support.

As quickly as possible, we ran off some portable fencing, topped up Omar's water supply, left a generous amount of hay to keep him amused then headed off down hill for accommodation, food and sleep.

Exhausted, hungry, stinking of horse and sweat, our choice of lodgings in Kinlochleven was bleak. At the first hotel I beat a hasty retreat. The smell of the whisky being poured for a local made my stomach wince. Even worse, in the warm ambient temperature, the lingering smells of old cooking oil coming from the kitchen extractor made me heave. On the second attempt, we initially thought that we had struck lucky. Although there were no rooms available in the main hotel, they did have "chalets" at the back. As it turned out these were little more than overgrown garden sheds with two sets of double bunks and nothing more. The showers and toilets were outside. But at least we had a bed for the night. In retrospect I should have opted for a night in the trailer. If the theory that Marc propounded earlier in regard to this anti-personality-counter-sense-of-humour mast started as a joke, by now this was becoming a harsh reality. The hotel bar and waiting staff were rude, discourteous; their manner couldn't care less. The food, a rubbery fish, wilted salad and greasy chips left a lot to be desired.

But they confidently knew that since most of the guests were in "chalets" or tents at the back, hill walkers seeking inexpensive accommodation, there was no necessity to provide anything more than basic facilities. Courtesy and hospitality were evidently outwith their pay grade.

With a day that approached some sixteen hours in duration, starting at Fenton Cottage near Rannoch Station, we clambered into the narrow bunks with the minimal headroom. Of course sleep was impossible. The chalet stifled with heat. There was too much noise. I was too wound up. My mind raced again over the problems on the West Highland Way at Altnafeadh and Kingshouse. I started to dwell on the subject. I worried about Omar up there on the hillside on his own. For a fleeting moment I thought about driving up to see if he was OK. That ensured that sleep or relaxation was unattainable. By one o'clock I decided to get up. As I walked outside every movement activated the sensors of each sensitive light I passed. I hastened across the grass to the toilet then just as hastily shot back to my bunk. Eventually I must have dozed off but all too soon woke up as Marc busied around preparing for breakfast. A shower, another plate of something that passed for food saw us on our way, hastily departing the makeshift accommodation as fast as humanly possible.

For the West Highland Way purists, the route starts at the roadside just past the school at Kinlochleven then works its way up through the woods to the open hillside of Stob Choire na'h Eirghe. It is a clearly marked route with magnificent views. For a time the track runs along the Alt na Thrath, on the opposite side of which Beinn na Caillich rises. The well maintained pathway rises and falls gradually until Tigh na-sleubhaich and Lairigmor are passed. The Way then contours the lower slopes of Meall a Chaorainn below which runs the tumbling waters of the Alt na Lairige

Moire. Finally the path drops down into the trees, which lead through to the junction at Blar a Chaorainn – our planned finishing point. The West Highland Way continues through the trees, descends into Glen Nevis then officially comes to a close somewhere near the visitor centre. As we walked down the track later that morning to rendezvous with the trailer, Omar showed no signs of any discomfort. But as a result of him spending the night in open hillside, the close proximity to sheep wool and damp ground, I decided in the morning that as we had to drive through Fort William anyway, a call to the vet might not be a bad thing. Any risk of exposure to infection had to be minimised. Marc was unwell, his stomach playing havoc. The casualties were starting.

I called the vet, explained what the problem was. Initially, I had wanted to meet the vet in the car park near the railway station where we would have plenty of room for vehicle and trailer. The vet had other plans. Instead he gave us directions to the surgery in Victoria Street, a narrow one–way thoroughfare that sits at the south east side of the town just above the main road through Fort William. My heart skipped a beat! As it transpired getting the trailer right next to the door of the practice was quite easy. I even managed to get parked in a spot where even with the front ramp down there was plenty of room, even though I wasn't keen to unload Omar unless absolutely necessary. The young vet came out to have a look. The remainder of the staff came out to have a look. A few cars stopped to have a look. Passers-by stopped to have a look. Omar stayed inside the trailer. The vet wanted the bandaging removed but refused point blank to get into the trailer. I agreed that there wasn't a lot of room but we were used to fitting travel boots and tail guards with Omar firmly locked into the breast and breech bars.

"But he might kick me," said the vet sheepishly.

"Well, he certainly won't kick me," I replied, knowing full well that I was correct.

I went into the trailer, took the scissors from the equine first aid kit and started removing the vet wrap. Omar didn't flinch. Marc stroked his nose. With the stretchy material removed, it was clear to see that the blood had dried on the gauze. I was going to have to remove this very carefully. Gently, very tenderly I slowly peeled off as much of the material as possible without disturbing the section over the actual cut. Marc fetched an apple and broke it into two pieces.

"When I say now, pop a bit of apple into his mouth," I instructed.

I reached for the strip of gauze.

"Now," pulling the remaining section off from the cut.

A piece of apple went into Omar's mouth. His foot rose up, foreleg twitched slightly and that was it. The vet was impressed; the various members of staff peeking sheepishly around the corner of the ramp were impressed. Marc and I just nodded. We knew Omar a lot better than that.

The senior partner popped his head around the side of the door, giving a cursory examination of the foreleg in the process.

"That's fine," he said, "seems to be healing nicely. You have done a good job".

His comments were appreciated. Then he went to say,

"Now if he as much as shows any sign of lameness in the next day, you must stop what you are doing immediately."

He instructed, and as an afterthought,

" Keep him away from as much wet, boggy ground as possible."

Him and me both, I mused.

The young vet still wanted Omar out of the trailer to treat and re-bandage the wound. So I led the horse out of the box, down the ramp along the street then on to the garage roof above the surgery building. There he stood, on top of a building, in a narrow street in the middle of Fort William.

The young vet still wasn't keen to get involved in the bandaging work; the close proximity to a horse's legs evidently wasn't his idea of fun. As it turns out horses were not a regular aspect of the practice, maybe the young vet simply lacked confidence. Actually I found the whole thing quite amusing but my confidence in Omar and his behaviour was unequivocal. So a veterinary nurse, herself a horse owner was drafted in to assist. As I held the head collar, Omar stood obediently as the two busied around, cleaning the wound, applying a new dressing then finishing it off with a cover of some bright red veterinary wrap. The vet prescribed some antibiotics and anti-inflammatory for a couple of days just to ensure that there was no risk of infection. Then with the medical work over, I walked Omar back up the street, and with the entire veterinary practice in attendance, watching like some entertained, yet fascinated audience, led him straight into the trailer. A few minutes later we were on our way to the Corran Ferry, but first a stop off for some quick late breakfast/lunch/brunch.

Fort William was bustling. At the supermarket parking was difficult, the entire area heaving, a plethora of large camper vans taking up double spaces. It is one thing parking a car in tight spaces, manoeuvring a loaded trailer is another but we soon found a space large enough for the Land Rover and trailer. Unfortunately as it transpired, the space was one of those discriminatory bays for Mothers and Toddlers. Typically, within seconds the guardian of the supermarket car park materialised as if by magic, checking numbers. Polite to the parking attendant, I explained that we would only be a few minutes and anyway Omar was only ten years old – still a toddler! The attendant, commented on the fine stature of my horse, laughed at my suggestion then walked away shaking his head. At least he had a sense of humour. With the few items collected from the store, we moved over to the McDonald's car park, to feast on some fast food as a "treat" for a late breakfast. My request for a hay burger for Omar fell on less than appreciative ears. No sense of humour there then!

For a short while we sat in the sun, eating the burgers, drinking coffee. With the food inside us, we felt marginally better. Occasionally, Omar looked out from the top hatch, interested in what was going on around him, then set his mind back to his hay net. Across the calm shimmering water of Loch Linnhe, the hills stood out, the sky clear but clouds were starting to roll in. It was time to move on. With the hatches closed up, we drove out of Fort William without a second thought; the brief exposure to the hustle and bustle was more than enough. From the centre we moved on to the A82, covering the short distance of four miles along a very busy road. In about twenty minutes we turned right towards the Corran Ferry loading ramp, joining a small queue of waiting cars. Ten minutes later we were parked on the small ferry, the thrum of diesels, noise from the single funnel, the swish of water permeating the peaceful crossing. Ten minutes after that, we were over the offload ramp, on to the terra firma of Ardnamurchan near Ardgour. The weather was holding. I felt a sudden burst of excitement run through me as finally we were now heading for the finishing line. To keep everyone at home advised I sent a single text.

"We are on the peninsula."

At the Edge of the World

*"The silent skies, an innocent heart, holding the
moment away from time in the dark"*

OR a few moments I gazed wistfully out over the rocky
finger of Corrachadh Mhor to the cold waters of the
Minch. The strengthening heat from the fast rising
sun to the east behind me was gradually burning off the
low-lying sea mist. Ever so slowly but discernibly the
horizon extended its way out over the Continental Shelf to
the North Atlantic. Coll was just visible to the south through
the haze but to the northwest Muck and the Small Isles had
yet to come into view. Directly west of me there was
nothing but a couple of thousand miles of cold grey ocean
between Canada's Newfoundland coast and where I stood.
In a fleeting moment I felt a sudden sense of isolation and
thought of home. Omar, standing quietly, patiently by my
side, chomped away at some tasty grass morsels and
seemed impervious to the surroundings.

As the sun poured more heat on to my back, I stared out
to the blue waters for a few more minutes. I was drained,
mentally and physically. My nerves were at breaking point
after the incessant pounding on the last few miles of
twisting, winding, single-track roads where the intense
concentration, constant alertness sapped physical and
mental well being. Although it was still early morning,
every corner, each blind summit demanded vigilance.

Muscles ached throughout my tired body. My eyes, protected by expensive sunglasses, stung through lack of sleep. My face was burned with the days of blistering sun, clothes stained with dried mud, flecks of blood, soaked through with sweat and stank of horse. But I was at peace surrounded in the tranquillity of the open ocean ahead of me, the stillness of the morning air. The only sound gentle waves lapping on the kelp covered black rocks below me.

Quietly satisfied, I chuckled to myself, occasionally chatting to Omar. Sipping on my drink, I proudly watched my horse, contently sniffing and picking at small bunches of grass. For some unknown reason he would give out an occasional but typical Arabian snort of disgust before continuing on his search for another equine treat. I reached my gloved hand out to his neck and stroked the fine smooth hair. Omar lifted his head and rested it on my shoulder. His warm breath brushed against my cheek as he nuzzled my face. I stroked his nose then looked into those deep dark eyes that probably belied a wisdom that few humans will ever know or understand. Together we had come a long road that was as much symbolic as it was physical and where each of us had been tried and tested on a number of occasions. Together we gave everything we had. We shared the scars, the cuts and bruises. When aching fatigue or dehydration burned deep we held on, heart, spirit, body and soul fused into one and we made it. Strangely, there was no immediate sense of achievement or elation. If anything I was in the usual neutral or unemotional state but in an untypical burst of philosophical thought, remembered bits of Kipling:

> *If you can force your heart and nerve and sinew*
> *To serve your turn long after they are gone,*
> *And so hold on when there is nothing in you*
> *Except the Will which says to them: 'Hold on!'*

It was almost exactly two years to the day since I had been carted out of Ward 4 in a wheelchair from the Acute Stroke Unit at Dundee's Ninewells Hospital, brain damaged, paralysed, emotionally wrecked and confused. My wife Rose took me home and guided me through the trauma to start the long, slow process to recovery. Days, weeks and months passed but gradually the frustrations, emotional ups and downs and the physical weaknesses receded as my strength and resolve returned. A newfound almost spiritual determination drove me on with tenacity.

Now, almost twenty-four months later I stood close to the most westerly tip of the Scottish mainland after having ridden a two hundred miles jog across the mountains and moors from the east coast. Very briefly I reflected back to that period of illness, the months of recovery then the aftermath and the duration of ruthless dedication and doggedness. Occasionally, those were difficult times. Sometimes the sheer physical pain and effort in constant training tested me to psychological and physiological breaking point. At times I probably became difficult to live with as I struggled to comprehend the mind reeling emotional roller coaster that I went through, endured although not alone. As personal loss and heartache came and went, the hard-bitten strength held firm, even though at times this took a further toll. But I was protected, wrapped in the love of my wife and daughters, those immediately close to me.

I had long since accepted that personal success is not an imaginary state of grace devoid of conflict, disappointment or frustration. Success is a journey not a destination but it has to be earned. Sacrifices have to be made, relationships tested, broken or strengthened. Finally came the culmination in the last few days of demanding, unrelenting and concentrated sheer physical and mental effort where trepidation or uncertainty held no place. As I stood with my horse at the edge of the world, on the last of the land, there was too much memory for my mind to comprehend. But relief, euphoria, a thousand pent up emotions from those strenuous days in the not too distant past suddenly flashed through my weary head. As the adrenalin started to leave my body I felt even more drained, numb but resisted any release of emotion to sweep over me. There was no urge; no need to let out great whooping cries of joy. A feeling of peace and tranquillity reigned. I looked back out to the serenity of those grey-blue waters and gently sighed. For a few moments longer I stood staring out over the Minch, letting the solitude wash over me. I felt nothing more than a sense of pride and humility.

Behind me, the rumble of the diesel engine and the clatter of the horse trailer snapped me back to reality. I looked over my shoulder to see Marc gunning the Land Rover towards us up the twisting turns of the final hill that brings the single-track road from Kilchoan to the start of the causeway to Ardnamurchan Lighthouse. Momentarily, I cast one final glance back towards Corrachadh Mhor, out to sea over the Minch then turned towards the Land Rover and trailer with Omar obediently following me. I led my horse around the edge of the grass; loyally he followed at my shoulder. I patted his neck, looked again into those deep dark mischievous eyes and thought of the mountains, moors, rivers and roads we had crossed together and smiled.

"Come on Omar, let's go home."

§

With the arrival onto the Ardnamurchan peninsula at Corran, the full realisation that the finishing line was ahead, although not quite in sight, lifted spirits. The first flushes of success were there but contained, held back. There was still a long way to go. Ardnamurchan is the long peninsula, which extends some twenty-eight kilometres west from Salen and Acharacle to the Point of Ardnamurchan, which is "almost" the most westerly point of the British mainland. It is not a mountainous region being for the most part rough undulating moorland which only in a few places rises highly and steeply enough to form recognisable hills. The attraction of Ardnamurchan is its remoteness, its fine coastline which in some places shows steep wild and rocky cliffs and in others placid sandy beaches. For many the remoteness of the region lies not only within its natural beauty and sense of isolation but in the almost inaccessible nature of the narrow twisting single track roads.

Now it was back to the mind numbing concentration needed on the miles and miles of those meandering single-track roads that lay ahead. With the exception of one portion of hill track that crosses to the north of Beinn na h-Urchrach the only way forward was by metalled roads. And metalled roads on the Ardnamurchan Peninsula, as good as the surface may be are not a welcoming experience for the unwitting motorist let alone a solitary horse and rider. The idea of hammering the horse along mile upon mile of monotonous road is something that never appealed to me but there were no alternatives. At least for the last leg of the journey and with the assistance of Kirsty Houston at Mingary and Liz Ford at Strontian an entire network of staging points and overnight stops that could break the monotony if need be had been set out. Our lines of communication were well and truly established. By the time we set foot and hoof on to the road towards Ardnamurchan and the last of the land, the entire peninsula knew were coming.

Strontian is a small hamlet that lies just beyond the junction between the A861 from Corran and the A884 to

Lochaline. The village is probably best known for the mines in the glen north of the village, The road to Loch Doilet hence to Polloch on the southern shores of Loch Sheil passes the largest of these mines which were recently reopened and there are now extensive workings. The mines originally dated from 1722 and were worked for lead until 1904 when they ceased production, then revived in the 1980s supplying barites for the North Sea oil industry. In 1764 the mineral *stontianite* was first found in these mines and from it the element *strontium* was discovered. If the hardships associated with extracting minerals from a harsh environment in the 18 [h] century were not enough, mining at the time had matters more problematic than exist today. A contemporary report suggests that "Highlanders" were stealing cattle, throwing sheep over precipices and setting fire to buildings. Terrorism at its most extreme! In response the unstoppable General Wade sent a sergeant and twenty men to help protect the owners interests.

From Strontian the route along the peninsula, is picturesque if nothing else. But the thing that makes this area, as with many in Scotland attractive to tourists or even those seeking to retire to peace and comparative solitude is the apparent remoteness. It was actually quite surprising just how many new and obviously expensive properties had been built. I assumed that these were the elaborate retreats of the retired well to do. The one thing for sure was that these were not the homes of the indigenous working population whose livelihoods were mostly centered on seasonal tourism and general estate work.

For most of the way the road lies in close proximity to the shores of Loch Sunart, which in turn snakes its way for approximately thirty-five kilometers between the Ardnamurchan and Morvern peninsulas. Just beyond the small island of Oronsay the sea loch finally opens out to eventually join the waters of the North Atlantic. On the north side of Loch Sunart, the road passes through sections of heavily wooded areas. Even on a bright day this section of the road was dark, claustrophobic and at times oppressive. In other places, the route lies in close proximity to the attractive sandy beaches and small coves that adorn the coastline where numerous yacht moorings, tucked into the sheltered bays, provided further pointers towards an absentee population.

Approximately twenty kilometres beyond Strontian the road passes through another heavily wooded area before skirting the wide bay at Salen. Then beyond the village the route then returns to its meandering path alongside the banks of Loch Sunart. As in many other places, with time to linger, it is a beautiful part of the west coast, sleepy, idyllic with stunningly beautiful scenery. It's a pity about the roads. Then maybe not! The biggest drawback on the twisting winding narrow road for horse and rider was the sheer concentration needed to try to anticipate what might be coming in the opposite direction. This makes it a slow, laborious but safe process. Given that the visibility beyond the tree-lined corners or minor summits was negligible, manoeuvring room even less, the idyllic scenery was relegated to a much lower order of importance. I don't particularly consider walking a horse is comfortable, preferring the faster working trot or even better a neat floating canter – but it was a case of needs must! Eventually after a further twelve kilometres beyond Salen the road snakes its way through the trees, crosses the burn, its source high above on the hillside at Lochan nam Fiann to pass through Glenborrodale. The area is named for the nomadic Viking, Borrodale, who settled in the area with his tribe. Buildings date back many hundreds of years. Throughout the length of the peninsula there are an overabundance of ancient sites

– chambered Cairns, Duns or remains that provide key indicators as to the various nationalities, invaders and settlers that influenced the area over the centuries.

Finally we reached the hill section just above the View-point near Ardslignish. The views out over the sea loch to the island of Mull then beyond to the Minch and North Atlantic were stunning. From there the road climbed stead-ily upwards to reach a few hundred metres above sea level. At this point the land was open, the barren moorland and rocky outcrops stretching out to be blocked by large sections of forestry plantations. Then beyond the tree lines, the land continued in undulating open moor, interspersed by further outcrops of gabbro. It was typical west coast terrain; hillsides rising almost straight out from sea level, but less pronounced than the imposing mountainsides of the far northwest. Finally as the route descended towards the coast again the sweeping mass of the open waters to the Minch could be seen to the west, across the sound, Ardmore Point on Mull stood out crystal clear. More importantly Kilchoan was now only three kilometers away. Just ahead of that at the end of a narrow rough farm track bounded on each side by coarse grass fields, stood the large outbuildings at Mingary. Gradually, steadily the day was coming to another welcome conclusion.

Donald Houston the beneficiary owner of Ardnamur-chan Estates personally made us welcome as we arrived at his estate headquarters at Mingary. The paddock for Omar had been set-aside in readiness, the bothy overlooking the bay offered to us for the night. Weariness was biting deep but with the best part of two hundred miles in the bag here was a chance to relax before the last final push for the most westerly point of the Scottish mainland. With Omar safely ensconced for the night in a huge grassy paddock just across the track from the bothy, Marc and I took a trip to Mingary

Pier near Kilchoan, topped up some provisions from the village shop then set about preparing our evening meal. As food burbled on the gas stove, stinking clothing was washed, and then hung out to dry, to adorn the fencing lines. A gentle breeze ensured that if nothing else, I would have a clean pair of socks to wear in the morning.

We dined well that evening. Sitting at the massive overly ornate carved bothy table we could see out to the bay then across the clear waters to Tobermory on Mull. With the food inside us, we felt better. We set about cleaning up, then organised the bits and pieces we would need for the next day. Just to ensure that the water would be hot for the early morning showers, I turned up to full blast what I thought was the thermostat for the water heater. Then for a while we wandered along the cliff tops, following the track down to the ruins of Mingary Castle. Across the sea loch, Tobermory could be seen in the evening sun, but its bright multi-painted houses along the front not quite visible from where we stood. Boats headed out to sea, others were headed towards Oban. Far to the west, the northerly tip of Coll was just visible as the bright orange sun sank towards its long day's end. The sea shimmered. At the castle we stopped to take a few photographs then stumbled across the old cannon that lies just to the north of the ruins.

Mingary Castle stands one and a half kilometers south east of Kilchoan. It is a fine ruined keep on the cliff edge overlooking the Sound of Mull. The castle's origins in the 13 [h] Century are obscure but for two or three centuries the MacIains of Ardnamurchan, close relatives of the Lords of the Isles, occupied it. At the end of the 15 [h] Century King James IV visited the castle twice to receive the allegiance of the island chiefs and a hundred years later withstood a siege by Spanish soldiers hence the name, Spanish Bay, *Port nam Spainteach*, for the little bay below the castle. Perhaps this had something to do with the wreck of the treasure laden Spanish galleon that is reputed to lie off the coast in Tobermory Bay. In 1644, Colkitto MacDonald, in support of King Charles I and Montrose took the castle from the Campbells who were then in occupation and withstood a siege by Argyll's army. However, the Campbells regained possession and were in Mingary at the time of the 1745 rising. The keep is now firmly under the ownership of Ardnamurchan Estate. It is highly unlikely that Donald and Kirsty who live in their modern property nearby have any use for the cannon as a means to withstand siege but the weapon lies as a constant reminder of the turmoil that played a pivotal role in the development of modern Scotland.

I had long since given up on a goods nights sleep, knowing perfectly well that tonight of all nights would be even more difficult. Tomorrow the ride would finish. Excitement, adrenalin coursed through me. I delayed the process of getting into my sleeping bag for as long as I could. Sleep could wait. Marc crashed out in the room next door but I lingered over more tea. For a while I read then convincing myself it was time for sleep crawled into my sleeping bag on the sofa couch. Taking long deep breaths, relaxing as best I could - nothing happened. Not only was the room beginning to get uncomfortably warmer but also the lack of curtains or blinds made sure that a steady stream of light poured into the room. With the temperature increasing, I kicked out of my sleeping bag.

As daylight diminished I must have fallen asleep, but was soon awake again, sweat pouring off me, my throat on fire, my eyes burning, and my mouth bone dry. I reached for the bottle of mineral water beside me, gulped down the contents. The curry was good but not that spicy, I mused. Then for a while I lay fully conscious this time in the darkness of middle night worrying I might have fallen foul of some devastating bug or worse still – food poisoning. Perhaps the insulation in the bothy was impressive? Obviously I was wrong. But fortune favours the brave. Typically, before I knew it, the first rays of a new dawn were breaking through the window just above me. With that I awoke. Hot! Thirsty! Bleary eyed, fevered and mouth as dry as the deserts of Saudi Arabia! The feeling was akin to being in an oven, slowly but systematically pot-roasted. The room was baking hot. There were no two ways about it – I had to get up.

Now the previous evening as we took stock of our temporary accommodation, one thing seemed to puzzle us. Our quest for a hot shower threw up one simple imponderable - hot water! We searched the accommodation throughout, but to no avail, seeking a switch or thermostat that would heat the water. Eventually we located a switch with a thermostat on the wall of the kitchen. What we couldn't find was any indication of central heating, radiators or otherwise. Therefore convinced that this was a water heater, I turned the unit to its very maximum. Half an hour later it appeared, that for all intents and purposes, the water was in fact slowly warming. Result! Now some twelve hours later, with stinging, puffy eyes rapidly dehydrating and soaked in sweat, marginally enthusiastic, I stepped out of the sofa bed. As my bare feet made the first contact with the tiled floor a fierce burning, scalding pain shot through them. I leapt into the air, cursing as loud as I could then landed back on the tiles. Cursing again, I carried out a sort of unimpressive pirouette to land crashing down on the sofa bed whereupon; my sleepy befuddled mind took stock of the situation, my eyes straying to the switch on the wall. The switch seemed to smile back at me – under floor heating. I reached for my boots but in the process fell off the bed on to the tiles.

"Ouch, oooooooooooyah, ouch," or words to that effect and groaned as the heat burnt at my bare legs.

Managing to retrieve one of my lightweight riding boots, fearful that the heat might melt the soles, I quickly hopped to the switch, turned it down, switched it off, forced open the windows then shot outside for a breath of cool morning air. Bliss! Thankfully, it was early morning, the place deserted. The sight of a semi-naked man wearing one riding boot and hopping on one foot outside the bothy may well have sent shockwaves throughout the Ardnamurchan Peninsula. Fearful of the media, my sense of responsibility overtook me. Just as quickly, I hopped back indoors. Entering the room from the cool morning atmosphere was the difference between walking from an efficient air conditioning system out into fifty-two degrees centigrade of Arabian Desert heat but in reverse. What I needed now was a lukewarm shower to cool me down. I quickly made some coffee then carried a mug through to Marc in the next room. The first thing I noticed opening the adjoining room door was the comfortable coolness of Marc's temporary accommodation. Still firmly ensconced in his sleeping bag on top of the hefty airbed, Marc was blissfully unaware of the blast of heat permeating the atmosphere from the next room.

"How come its nice and cool in here?" I asked, proffering the mug of coffee.

"Don't know," he replied sleepily, "but I turned that switch thing on the wall there off last night."

I took my coffee then went back outside to gulp in the fresh morning air - and screamed.

Suitably cooled down, I walked out to the paddock to feed an eager Omar who had taken to exploring the far corner of the field. On sight of his feed bucket he immediately dispensed with his curiosity for neighbouring land, his canter towards me coming to an abrupt stop as the purple bucket was placed next to the water trough. As usual Omar seemed totally unfazed by his overnight stop, munched his breakfast in a genteel manner then wandered off to explore a little further. Back at the bothy we prepared an equally high octane yet hasty breakfast, packed up the equipment then retrieved Omar from the far reaches of his temporary realm. As I led Omar down the track towards the steadings, the sun broke out over the hills to the east. For a further day the weather prediction seemed correct. For another day Team Omar was eager to go.

With Omar tacked we bid our thanks to Donald Houston, passing on my regards to his wife Kirsty who had been instrumental in making the passage and logistics along the peninsula so much easier. As the clock ticked onwards we then set off along the narrow track from Mingary to the junction just east of Kilchoan. The plan for the day was to finish at the lighthouse then ride back to Glenborrodale, a round trip of about forty-five kilometers. With this in mind, the trailer was left next to the steading at Mingary where it would be picked up on the return leg. Marc would follow on in the vehicle carrying the small items that might be needed, including water containers slosh bottles, sponges and food. Able to dispense with a bum-bag and the para-phernalia that it contained, I stripped down to my light-weight riding clothes and fluorescent bib. For the last part of the ride, I fully intended to be as comfortable, light and as visible as possible. Even if the weather did break, at least our back up would only be a few hundred metres away.

It was still very early morning as we trotted out on to the single-track road. Even if I had slept badly for a further night, there was not any sense of fatigue. Perhaps the adrenalin was starting to build up, my mind fully conscious and that barring incidents, within an hour or so we would be in view of the "almost" most westerly tip of the Scottish mainland. For some reason, I expected the lighthouse to be visible the minute we passed the junction just outside Kilchoan that led to the pier – Cidhe Chille Chomhghain. The signpost, strangely worded did at least appear to show the way.

FOR ARDNAMURCHAN POINT
FOLLOW LIGHTHOUSE

But as we passed into the village the only thing that I could see ahead of me were hills, and pretty steep ones at that. I was disappointed, expecting the lighthouse to loom into view at any minute, to act as a final target. At the church I carefully manoeuvred Omar past the strings of balloons, bunting and flags that adorned the roadside in preparation for the society wedding that I knew was about to take place later that day. I didn't want to be responsible for upsetting the layout of the decorations nor did I wish Omar to adorn the roadside with a miniature mountain of manure. Anyway I convinced myself. Then I conjured up an impression of the newly weds or guests rushing out of the church – no don't even think about it. Biting my gloved finger suppressed the hysterical fit of giggles that was about to burst forth. Instead I focused harder on the road ahead but just in case I made a cursory glance backwards - all clear!

About five hundred metres past the village church the road split at a V-junction, one route leading to the old township of Ormsaigbeg by the shore, the other route pointing to Portuairk, Sanna and Ardnamurchan Lighthouse. It was around about this point that Omar characteristically deposited his trademark at the side of the road. At least the wedding party would be safe. We quickly swung right on to the next section of road, passing a final line of properties where a young horse careered over the field, grossly overexcited at the sight of another equine. As we neared the end of the field, I politely steadied Omar to a gentle walk, whereby his only reaction being a haughty glance at the youngster. The young horse went ballistic. Behind me I could hear an angry owner screaming at the horse. I quickly glanced back, ignored the commotion then selfishly focused back on my own task in hand. Nothing to do with me!

By now we were nicely warmed up. Omar was ready to go. When the open countryside reared into view - we clicked up a gear. As we climbed out of Kilchoan upwards to Lochan no Crannaig, the last vestiges of the Sound of Mull disappeared, blocked by the hills of Stacan Dubha and Beinn an Seilg. On each side there was nothing but miles of open moorland stretching away northwards to the minor range of the Meall an Tarmachain hills. Small rocky outcrops stood out against the darker colour of the heather clad hillsides. Here the rock is principally gabbro, the region having been once the site of a great volcano. The last vent of the volcano can be identified as an insignificant little knoll midway between Achnaha and Glendrian, six kilometers north-north west of Kilchoan. This knoll is at the centre of a plain about four kilometers diameter and surrounded on all sides except one by low lying gabbro hills, the only gap in the ring being the valley of the Allt Sanna on the north west. There is a good deal of bare rock in the western half of Ardnamurchan and the hills which are mostly grassy on their lower slopes have gabbro outcrops on their crests. Vegetation was sparse, the heather still showing the dark brown wasted colour of winter. But the first growth of spring was starting to show. At the roadside, coarse grass, patches of moss provided easy pickings for the flock of sheep that started to follow us, their rumps painted with a bright blue splash.

As we passed Loch na Crannaig, its still water thick with weed, rushes and the shoots of water lilies to come, all that could be seen ahead were hills. In the distance the single-track road curved beyond, contouring the hillside. Of the lighthouse there was still no sign. As each blind corner or minor summit was passed, I continued to expect the whitewashed structure to come into view. Each occasion I was disappointed. I had no need of a map but was keen to determine just where I was. But as the road gradually dropped down into the small woods near the Sonnachan Hotel, my dead reckoning reasoned that we were about three and a half kilometers or twenty minutes away from the finish line. As the road led steeply downwards, Omar took the descent steadily, placing one foot carefully, calculating his steps. Even in the dry conditions, patches of the metalled surface were shiny, no place for a skid. Each corner, every blind summit now demanded that little bit more concentration as the traffic started to flow a little more intensely. For the nth time, a black 4x4 passed us. Each time, the same miserable faced driver seemed oblivious to anyone else on the road. Later he would pass for a final time, his wedding attire clearly visible through the windscreen. Perhaps he was the father of the bride preparing to give his daughter away. I would have thought that the knowledge in that would have cheered him up.

For some of the time, I could either see cars coming from a distance or at least hear them. This gave ample warning to move Omar closer into the verge when it was safe to do so. But for most of this section of roadwork, the continuous blind corners or summits ensured that a constant vigilance was necessary. At least with the Land Rover a few hundred metres behind me, protecting me from any unwary motorists hurtling up behind, I could concentrate on what was happening ahead. Nearing the Sonnachan Hotel, my first instinct was to stop for a mug of coffee, but resisted the temptation. We pressed on up the next long hill, passing the woods left and right reaching the junction at Achosnich where the signposts provided a final indicator to our destination.

At this point we happened upon the walker, an elderly gentleman out for a ten-kilometre morning constitutional. For a few minutes we walked alongside him, chatting about his daily walking routine, his zest for exercise in the fresh air. He seemed fascinated by the entire concept of the Trans Scotland. When I mentioned the fund raising for the Acute Stroke Unit he waited for the Land Rover to catch up then collected a form from Marc. Just as the road commenced a further downward section, the walker was left behind. At the cattle grid ahead of me near Grigadale, Marc quickly opened the gates to let us through.

With less than a kilometre to go now, there was still no sight of the lighthouse but what I could see in the distance was the North Atlantic, its blue grey waters covered by a low lying sea mist. As we trotted around the bends just past Grigadale, the road dropped slowly towards the coast then sea level. As I stared out to the ocean ahead, disappointment grew as momentarily I imagined that the mist was moving towards us, threatening to block out an otherwise beautiful day. But I was wrong.

It seemed just like two years ago and there I was again, riding with the light. Ahead of me was mist. But this time it was nothing more than low cloud over the sea, no eerie shapes darted around. On one side of me the low ground fell away to the rocky foreshore, *machair*. On the other side the ground climbed slowly over broken rock towards heather covered hillsides, extending out over the vast moorland beyond which forms the Ardnamurchan Penin-sula. There was no dark tunnel, no shadowy beings in the hazy peripherals. Behind me the sun was rising fast, bursting through the weak clouds to explode in brilliant light. We picked up speed as each corner; each minor summit now brought us closer to the final destination. I didn't turn once but could feel the warmth on my back, sensed again the shafts of rainbow light that were bursting around me. Ahead the sea mist was rolling off the blue waters, sunlight sparkling off the waves. This was no dream, no illusion or distortion of a befuddled mind and damaged brain. This was reality. Behind was light; ahead was the end of a road that had started somewhere two years ago in the sub consciousness of a bewildered mind.

The last section of single-track road that leads from Kilchoan to the start of the causeway to Ardnamurchan Lighthouse and Visitor Centre is a gentle gradient with twisting curves. We trotted on, each step a little closer to finishing. Although I still couldn't see a lighthouse what I did see ahead of me was a car parked at the side of the road. Next to that was what looked like a stone bridge, oddly enough adjacent to that was a set of traffic lights. And the lights were at red! For a moment I was confused, my mind struggled to solve the significance. Then it dawned on me. We were at the end of the short causeway that leads along the edge of the small cliffs and foreshore to the lighthouse itself. Obviously, as the causeway was narrow, the traffic lights were in place to prevent vehicles meeting in the middle of a narrow road. The other thing that did immediately catch my eye was the big bright blue and white painted sign that gushed out its welcome.

WELCOME TO
ARDNAMURCHAN POINT
VISITOR CENTRE

Just to the south the rocky finger of Corrachadh Mor, the most westerly point on the British mainland thrust out to the sea, gentle waves lapping against the black kelp covered rocks. To the right of the painted sign, one more item of man made intrusion caught my eye. And that was a cattle grid with no obvious means of getting past. Well we were almost there. Did a few more metres really make that much difference? According to Marc when the vehicle caught up with us, it did. So we set about finding a way through. On the coastline side was a steep rock embankment leading down to the shore - effectively impassable. On the opposite side of the causeway there was a narrow gate in the wall but right alongside this was a wooden post that ensured that it would have been impossible to get Omar safely through avoiding the slats of the cattle grid.

As the walkers on the West Highland Way had taken hearty kicks at the fence posts near Altnafeadh, I took a booted swipe at this post. In doing so, the post resisted any attempt at lodgement; instead I skidded to land very firmly on my rear end, gashing my arm in the process. In frustration, I lashed out again but the fence post held firm. I was ready to call it a day. Together we assessed the situation. Marc headed to the lighthouse in the search for some solid boards that we could use to bridge the slatted grid but returned empty handed. There was nothing we could do. Except! Marc suggested that he drive back to Mingary, pick up the trailer then use that to get Omar across the grid. So that was agreed. Leaving me at the end of the causeway with a cup of coffee from the Visitor Centre tearoom, Marc headed off.

As we waited for Marc to return, I sipped on my coffee, chatted to the odd passers-by, cyclists, drivers intrigued by the fact that I was standing at the end of the causeway with a horse. They seemed reluctant to believe my responses when I replied that I wasn't quite sure why either. Typically, Omar chomped at the grass, haughtily aloof. At this point in time, I had no immediate flushed feeling of success or achievement. In a sense I remained impartial to the conclusion that was now only minutes away. For a while I stared wistfully out to the waters of the Minch and beyond that the North Atlantic. It had been a remarkable trip and I was quietly proud, pleased with the achievement. But there was something else.

§

When Kirsty Graham won the Scottish Endurance Championships at Scone on the diminutive Arabelle she coined a phrase that should be indelibly engraved in every endurance riders psyche. Kirsty said that there is not a word in the English language that means "proud and humble" at the same time. She is right and there probably should be. That's how I felt – proud and humble. Proud of what had been achieved not only by me but those around me that had helped to make this happen. Humble – very much so, humbled by everything that I had seen around me, the scenery, the history and the culture of proud ordinary people that had travelled much of this way before me. But most of all I was immensely proud of my slightly built horse, humbled by the courage, determination, strength and spirit of a true son of the four winds.

I stroked Omar's neck, my gloves running over the smooth coat. As he rested his head on my shoulder, I looked into those deep expressive eyes. As always that sparkling twinkle of worldliness amused me and I wondered just what he might have been thinking. For a few moments I looked back out to sea, reflecting on the last two years but more so on the experiences of those last few days. Any bitterness that might have lingered over the illness had long since passed. There are no recriminations. What happened - happened. Nothing in the past can be changed only a willingness to mould the future. Everyone is filled with a sense of loss, tragedy or personal failure sometime in his or her life. I am no exception, certainly not special. The main difference between those who succeed in life and those who fail is the knowledge of how to get back up. There has to be a degree of arrogance, brutal determination and rigid doggedness. Maybe that attitude can be misinterpreted. Sometimes, I knew perfectly well that being confident and having a positive attitude would not solve my problems but if those traits annoyed enough people then it was worth it. When the icy tentacles of pious Calvinism are allowed to squeeze on the heart it must be difficult to retain that air of confidence. It's a pity about the Scot's crisis of confidence but it is a very Scottish trait – confidence and success to be frowned upon, almost feared – always someone ready for the inevitable "put-down". Either way we now stood at the last of the land having beaten the odds, tired maybe but proud and humble?

John Grierson probably sums it up best for me when he said. The secret of it is that we are a peasant and a proletarian people and have never had courtly affairs to strait jacket us. Our songs are the songs of the common people, our practicality is of a people with a living to make, and a daily job to do, and no fine airs to impose on anybody. We never had anything but what we got out of our common doings as working people. It's a set of values to be immensely proud of. And being proud of our achievements is commendable. There is no shame in that. But as Hugh MacDiarmid said, "There is no necessity whatsoever to indulge in any airs and graces. Pomp and circumstance, frippery, finery, posh words, anything that can be dismissed as all meringue and nae mince is easily suspect in Scotland as it suggests pretension – the desire to pretend that you are something you are not." We had taken a job in hand, carried it through with the minimum of fuss, no blaze of publicity, no fanfare, no aspirations other than to finish what we set out to do. And that was the end of it.

The battle for recovery is still there. Perhaps it might be forever? Who knows? Some days are tough but for the rest of the time life is marvellous. Oh the blinding headaches come and go, the sickness generated by a range of medicine will linger indefinitely but that I suppose is a small price to pay. Sometimes inside my head the befuddled remnants of a brain damaged mind cause problems. Some days my concentration lapses, many times where there is a need to be emotional there is a void. Occasionally, it can be difficult to function in circumstances where loud noise or groups of chattering people are around me. Partial dyslexia is an added complication. The weakness in hand and ankle still lingers - probably will forever but I have compensated for that.

If nothing else I have learned that fears can be overcome, apprehensions overthrown, however hard that might be to achieve, and maybe we are all just catapulted along a direction over which we may have little control. Horses are no longer big scary things but beautifully expressive and loyal friends, without one my life may well have been a whole lot different. I also know and understand that endurance within any sport or at any level is a whole lot more than just chugging a horse around sign-posted berry fields. It takes confidence, effort, focus, determination and a huge amount of deliberate practice. And that can hurt! As for the limits of endurance – well? Some mathematicians and physicists would argue – there is no such thing.

§

Behind me the rumble of the diesel engine and the clatter of the trailer snapped me out of my philosophical musings. I looked back to see Marc swinging the vehicle up the last slope and final bend on the road from Kilchoan. Within minutes we had Omar loaded then crossed the cattle grid. A few minutes later I stood with my horse below the huge grey stone structure with its whitewashed buildings that guards the rocks of the "almost" most westerly tip of the British mainland – Ardnamurchan Lighthouse.

For about thirty minutes I basked in the day. Like some very proud father, I paraded Omar around the car park now filling with a crowd of tourists. Numerous people of all walks approached us, photographing Omar against the backdrop of the lighthouse. Many were intrigued about the journey; many gave small donations of money for the fundraising in aid of the Acute Stroke Unit at Dundee's Ninewells Hospital. A few people, just as the walker did, took forms away for completion, promising to help raise further funds. We never saw any of those forms back or any of the monies promised. It didn't matter. Somewhere back in the steep hillsides of the Cairngorms, I had long since given up on the idea that this was about sponsorship.

The remainder of the day became a whirlwind. From the lighthouse we beat as fast and as hasty a retreat as possible or as much as the long twisting roads of the peninsula would allow us. At Kilchoan we narrowly escaped bumping into the wedding party but as I passed I quietly wished them well. From there we backtracked to Glenborrodale over the top of Beinn Hiant to arrive at the gates of the imposing Glenborrodale Castle. The Castle as it is today was built in 1900 when a Mr C D Rudd, a wealthy magnate of De Beers association who made his fortune in the diamond mines of South Africa, bought the estate and became laird of Ardnamurchan. During the construction work a hundred local men who daily walked the 13 miles from Kilchoan were employed at a weekly wage somewhere at the equivalent of £1.25.

The work took some three years to complete and according to local legend, before he passed away Mr Rudd buried a large diamond somewhere in the grounds. The Stables house beside the castle is three hundred years old and the castle itself stands on the site of the original mansion house, built for the owner of Ardnamurchan Estate. As I walked around the castle grounds to the front of the building, I glimpsed into an opulent interior. It would have been easy to imagine, if inclined, oneself back in the days of glamour and opulence when lavish house parties were the rage. At the castle Chris showed us the area of paddock complete with an equally opulent field shelter for Omar then left us to sort out the fencing and water supplies. At that juncture I could have quite happily crawled into my sleeping bag atop the diminishing bales of hay and slept until dawn.

Our trip to Strontian later that afternoon in search of fuel brought about an abrupt change of plans. For the first time in two days I managed to get a very brief mobile signal, with it a message from Liz Ford at Anaheilt. Accommodation was ready for us at the croft, a paddock arranged for Omar. The opportunity was too good to pass up. We made an immediate about turn. This of course meant another laborious trail along the twisting single-track roads but the plus side was that we could leave straight from Strontian first thing in the morning. Within two hours we had packed up the electric fencing, loaded Omar and relocated to Strontian. With the horse safely turned out for the night, rugged up, sprayed with insect repellent we returned to the comfortable croft then set about finding somewhere to eat.

A short time later as I sat down at the well laid out tables and chairs of the attractive timber built restaurant at Ariundle, still clad in riding gear, probably smelling a bit, the realisation and relief washed over me. We chinked glasses, toasted the ride then fed on a veritable feast of superb home cooked, local produce. There was a lot to be said that night as the benefits of civilisation returned. We had lost more than the best part of two days through the loss of the shoe, the impromptu visit to the vet, along with added detours forced on us but the plan had held. Despite some issues, which we had overcome quite efficiently, the objective had been completed. And as I sipped on a second beer, relaxed, now free of the pressure to chase a record, undoubtedly relieved, probably just starting to get a tad intoxicated, the sudden realisation of achievement finally washed over me with a body draining – whoosh. The only thing I wanted now was to get home.

For the first time in four nights, I slept well. In fact the excellent meal at the Ariundle Centre, coupled with a few beers, three I think, or was it four, left me soporific, slightly tipsy. By nine o'clock that evening as the sun sank over the western islands I was unconscious. Nine hours of solid undisturbed sleep later I woke up, rested, relaxed, ravenously hungry and desperate to get home. As we woke that morning it was to a grey misty world of low cloud and drizzle. The slight rain pattered on the windows, the trees across the drive obscured by a low-lying mist.

With a good nights rest behind us and a hearty breakfast inside, we set about packing up ready for the long road journey ahead. Omar was caught up from Liz Ford's spacious field just along the road from her croft. With his breakfast inside him, we fitted him out for the long trailer ride ahead. Satisfied that he was comfortable in his rigid travel boots, tail guard and travel fleece and with enough hay in the nets to keep him occupied we lashed down the rest of the tack and equipment on the other side the trailer.

The morning remained damp but humid. As Marc dragged the water containers up from the burn, for the first time throughout the entire traverse of Scotland, the midges attacked - vigorously! Within minutes insect repellent was swishing the air but the regimented swarms of infamous flying demons continued to home in with all the skill of laser guided weaponry. The elderly Postmistress at Achilti- bue was right when she once told me – midges are put on earth to prove that man is not the dominant species. Losing the battle, we quickly closed up the trailer hatches then beat a hasty retreat to the internal security of the Land Rover.

We reached the Corran Ferry within thirty minutes. At Ardour we joined the queue waiting for the ferry that took us back on to the mainland just south of Fort William. The sea loch was choppy, the skies growing black with thicken- ing clouds. The days of glorious sunshine and blistering heat seemed to have passed by now. The weather had finally broken. Dark clouds loomed over the hills to the south and west, the increasing wind throwing the sea loch into a heaving chop. The ferry swung in a calculated S shape over Loch Linnhe as the skipper negotiated the tide and wind. Within minutes we had docked at the mainland jetty, the offload ramp clattering down. As we passed the queue of cars waiting to cross, people started to gesture and point. Car after car full of people stared as the vehicle and trailer climbed up the slope and passed. And each one waved. It was puzzling but a welcome gesture.

For the next seven hours we headed home along the monotonous twisting roads and constant traffic. The civili- sation of transportation was all too abrupt. At Blair Atholl, we stopped at the castle; Marc collected his car then we parted company. A couple of hours later, I gently swung the vehicle and trailer into the narrow road leading to the yard, passing Omar's paddock on the left. The journey that had taken a number of days on horseback had taken a matter of eight hours to get home. It was good to be back.

Very soon people, friends, family started to arrive. Livery owners passed, going about their business but stopped to give me their regards. There were welcome smiles, hugs, and a bottle of champagne. More importantly for me the one person that matters most in my life was there to see us home, my wife Rose, eyes brimming with pride, the knowing look that said everything, the gentle smile - in her hand the bunch of red roses.

As an increasing throng of people gathered around Omar in admiration he merely focussed his attention on the packet of mints in my jacket pocket. Satisfied that there were no further treats forthcoming he turned his attention to his hay. Then in a manner befitting the true professional, the real cool dude that he truly is, he switched off. As a thank you, I picked a single flower from the bunch and tied it on Omar's stall. Team Omar was safely home. The run for the roses was over.

> *"And it's run for the roses*
> *As fast as you can*
> *Your fate is delivered*
> *Your moments at hand*
> *It's a chance of a lifetime*
> *In a lifetime of chance*
> *And its high time you joined in the dance."*

And we did!

Postscript

"Would it be a waste? Even if I knew my place,
to leave it there?"

URING the course of the Trans Scotland we climbed
and descended something in the region of 12,000
feet of extremely varied terrain. The distance from
the east to west coasts of Scotland was covered in a riding
time of forty-nine hours, thirty-four minutes and twenty-six
seconds. The walkers of The Great Outdoors Challenge
starting the chase from the west coast at the same time as
we departed from Scurdie Ness never really did stand a
chance! Anyway, I didn't for one minute actually believe
that they ever would.

For a couple of weeks after getting home, despite being
remarkably fit and healthy I felt drained, lost, chronically
fatigued and seemed to wander around aimlessly. There
was nothing really wrong with me, it was apparently a
perfectly ordinary response to winding down; the body and
mind making the adjustments necessary to get back to a
more conventional routine existence without the continuous
daily boost of adrenalin. I suppose in a basic street sense I
was undergoing a rather abrupt episode of "cold turkey"!!

Strangely enough though, I never really did feel any
necessity or haste to seek out or bask in any sense of
recognition. Instead I just remained quietly proud, indubi-
tably humble, constantly amused by the entire episode and

modestly embarrassed by the occasional media attention thrust on me. When I started riding just over eighteen months previously I religiously followed my belief in that there were no aspirations for greatness, no quest for ego boosting falsehoods. And I still believe that. It had just seemed the right thing to do at the time – a human thing, doing what seems right, not what is easy. But then other priorities did take over. Within a couple of weeks we commenced the beginning of our competitive endurance career, *chasing pavements*. Then over the following months we would move progressively and quite rapidly from an Endurance Great Britain Novice towards Advanced combination. Inevitably I did find out rather quickly and abruptly, the accuracy behind what the American endurance rider Suzy Kelley rightly said, ". . . it can be all the nasty things in the world, but it's still fun!" As Candy Cameron said to me, "We don't make mistakes in endurance riding, we just get lessons to learn from. Remember that!"

§

A short time later I gave a talk on the Trans Scotland in response to the invitation from the Camperdown Rotary Club. At the same time, I handed over a cheque for the monies we had raised for the Acute Stroke Unit at Ninewells to Ron McWalter, President of the branch and hospital consultant. It wasn't a huge amount of cash; the donations gathered from a wide range of people were still generous. But in some small way I hope that it goes to help the people from all walks of life, young and old who have been crippled by a horrible illness. Perhaps it will assist the doctors and nurses and staff who work so tirelessly to care for the sick. It was the least that I could do. My additional and unexpected reward for that was a family invitation to the Queens Garden Party at Holyrood Palace.

§

Jarrow was retired to a lovely location where he over-looks the Perthshire countryside and the river that flows past the foot of his paddock. Every so often he is taken for a gentle amble through the woods and surrounding land. He gave a lifetime of service and deserves his well-earned rest. Whenever possible, I take a walk into the hills of Glen Lethnot and climb up to the steep slopes of Craig Duchray. At the place where I had scattered the ashes of my Springer Spaniel, I leave a single flower and pause for a spell of meditative peace and tranquillity. There will always be a place in my heart for those two loyal animals.

§

On one cold February afternoon the following year, I searched around for a suitable gift for my wife. Somewhere along the way I bought the obligatory flowers and choco-lates for that particular Valentines Day. However, as Rose came through the patio doors that evening she was some-what surprised to be met, well actually almost knocked over by a rather boisterous, exuberant, but now completely devoted chocolate coloured German Shorthaired Pointer officially called Erlau Fontwell. Thankfully, he is known as Jack.

"Whose dog is that?"

Honestly, I did buy the flowers and chocolates first!!

§

As usual life goes on and all too soon we were back in more familiar terrain. All around me horses, riders, crew bustled about. Officials scurried here and there as final preparations were made, vehicles rolled out to the check-points and crewing points. After a week of torrential rain, it was inevitable that the 40kms course would be tough. But as usual we were prepared to dig that little bit deeper, always ready to go down to the wire if necessary.

I walked Omar around for a few minutes then headed for the timekeeper. As the countdown started, my mouth as usual went bone dry. It was another day, another challenge, another competitive endurance ride and life was good. Unknown to me at that point in time and some two hundred odd miles away, a gorgeous little baby girl with a heart-melting smile had made a sudden and quite dramatic entrance into the world. As Cayla Rose was taking her first breaths in a new dawn, her proud grandfather, totally unaware of the arrival of the new family addition, nudged his pure bred Arabian gelding over another start line that morning. Life was about to turn upside down all over again. Another chapter was about to open.

All of a sudden the words of the occupational therapist that had assessed me in hospital the morning I was discharged, came crashing back.

"You know with time and rehabilitation, a third of people will make a fairly full recovery physically, and should be encouraged to lead a normal life."

Reflecting on that thought, I almost burst into hysterical laughter.

"C'mon Omar – lets go." And as usual he needed no second telling!

A normal life?